Pathways to Health
An Integral Guidebook

PATHWAYS TO HEALTH
an Integral Guidebook

INCLUDES:
THE MAP YOUR HEALTH
MISSION DESIGNER

Victor Acquista, M.D.

Mill City Press, Inc.
212 3rd Avenue North, Suite 290
Minneapolis, MN 55401
612.455.2294
www.millcitypublishing.com

The material presented in this book is based upon the research and opinions of the author. It is not presented as a substitute for consulting with your physician or other health care provider to address your health care needs. Diagnosis and treatment should be done in conjunction with health care professionals.

ISBN-13: 978-1-935204-94-7
LCCN: 2013900043

Cover Design and Typeset by Steve Porter

Printed in the United States of America

Dedication

This book is dedicated to all those who seek a better understanding of what lies within.

Acknowledgments

Many people contributed to the creation of this guidebook. To acknowledge them all would simply not be possible. I would be remiss not to single out my friend, Paul Schnaittacher, for his superb photography. I give special thanks to my family, friends, mentors, and patients who have helped me come to a better understanding of health and healing. I am further grateful for the many fellow travelers who have shared aspects of their personal journeys with me, allowed me to travel with them, and have helped me move forward on my own path to better health. I have deep gratitude and appreciation for all you have given and continue to give to me.

The chains that bind us…
are self-forged

Table of Contents

Preface

I don't have the answers to your health problems, but I do have the questions. The standard Western view of health doesn't have the answers either. In many respects, conventional medicine doesn't even ask the right set of questions. The same applies to alternative, complementary, and integrative approaches to care. Despite claims to the contrary, none are truly holistic and all these approaches are fragmentary. In the pages that follow we shall discuss health and the means to achieve better health. As we journey through life we are constantly faced with choices. In a sense, these choices represent intersections and forks in the road. We can observe many interesting things as we travel down any path. Sometimes we reach a dead end. Sometimes we choose the wrong path and need to circle back. Some of our choices take us down old familiar roads. Other times we find ourselves on unfamiliar ground or in places we prefer not to be. If there is a particular destination we have in mind, it is often helpful to have a map, or some good directions to help us get to that particular place. Without a map or some familiarity with the territory we tend to get lost. We can waste a lot of time stumbling around lost, with no clear direction to go.

So much today is written about health. We all have our own personal and family experiences about health and illness which affect our judgment and perception. We are inundated and assaulted by information and advertising about health. Should I take a vitamin? If so, what kind? How much exercise should I be doing? What are the best foods to eat and what is the best diet for me? These are questions people ask themselves, their friends, and their doctors all the time. Doubtless, we all would like to be healthy. But is the secret to good health simply eating the right foods, getting proper exercise, and taking the right supplement? Faced with a myriad of choices, people all too often become discouraged. Frequently they try one strategy and if they don't find themselves feeling great, they soon embark on a new strategy. How many health fads, new scientific breakthroughs, fancy diets, pills, and alternative medicine approaches have you been exposed to during your lifetime? How many have you embraced? How many more are on the way? How many have promised more energy, a better sex life, a longer life and how many have actually delivered on these claims?

I am not carte blanch criticizing various strategies which people follow to attain a more healthy life. There are merits in many different approaches. I do add my voice to those who criticize our current approach to health as fragmented. Although there are many excellent sub specialists and alternative medicine practitioners, no single health care practitioner receives training in evaluating each person in an individualized truly holistic manner. This results in a plethora of different practitioners focusing in on their particular narrow area of training and expertise. It is easy to lose sight of the forest when you are only focused on a few trees. I am not so presumptuous to claim I have secret knowledge to share with you which will guarantee you more energy, better sex, or a longer life. But I am absolutely certain that you can enjoy good health. I am absolutely certain that with proper guidance and thoughtful understanding about making the right choices that you can travel a pathway to health.

In the pages that follow you will be presented with a conceptual framework which outlines the territory of your health. The answers you give to the questions I ask will enable you to fill in the landscape details and enable you to create a map. With this map, you can choose your pathway to health.

A guide is someone who knows the territory—someone who can help us get through especially difficult terrain. A guide knows the roads and paths traveling through a particular area. He or she knows that there are many ways to get from point A to point B. Some of these ways may be straightforward while others might be rather circuitous. A good guide will point out features along the way. Sometimes these are hazards or pitfalls; other times these may be particularly scenic areas or points of beauty. The best guides will also assist the traveler in bringing along the necessary equipment to ensure a successful journey.

PREFACE

I would like to be your guide as we travel together. I know from choices I have made in my own life how some have brought me to places of better health and some have not. I know from having the privilege of being a primary care physician how people struggle to be healthier. An integral approach is very comprehensive. It demands a highly individualized perspective for each person that recognizes the unique characteristics of that person which affect health and well-being. Only you can create the individualized map which details the territory of your health. While each of us has a unique map, we all share a common capacity to heal ourselves. In the integral approach, the healer becomes a facilitator, who guides you through a process which allows healing from within. This inner healing is available to all. It's available to you; although, you may need a little help to navigate the way. Allow me to be your guide as we walk together to take your pathway to health.

Pack light, bring an open mind, and enjoy the journey…

Photo courtesy Paul Schnaittacher

Introduction

VIDEO LINK #1 IN APPENDIX

Mary Perkins is seated in the chair next to my examination table as I enter the room. A hard working single woman in her forties, she is here today to follow up on her diabetes. I always marvel at how she manages to work her grueling job and care for her ailing mother. As I extend my hand for a customary handshake I can immediately sense that something is wrong.

"Hi, Mary how have you been doing?"

A worried frown replaces her normal big smile, "Oh, doctor, I've been bad! I've been eating all the wrong things."

"Hmmm!" I exclaim, "Normally you are so good with your diet and your blood sugars have been excellent. Is everything okay with your mother?"

"No, it's not my mother, she's the same. I…, I…." Somehow the words get stuck in her throat and tears well in her eyes.

"I got laid off from work and I just don't know what I'm going to do!"

She's not alone. I'm not sure what to do either, but we spend the whole visit discussing her situation and charting a course to get her diabetes, and in a real sense her life, back to a place of better health.

Johnny Gerard wheels himself away from the swinging examination door as I enter. Although he is now in his early 50's everyone still calls him Johnny boy. His aging parents are also patients of mine. I am always inspired by my encounters with him. Although paralyzed by a diving accident during his youth, he seems to have excelled in life. A successful accountant, he also enjoys a happy long term marriage, and a couple of children that he never tires of talking about.

"How's it going, Johnny boy?"

"Hey doc, same old, same old." He is smiling as he lifts himself unassisted onto the exam table.

"Any trouble with your bladder?" Johnny has to self-catheterize in order to empty his bladder. The damage to his spinal cord as a result of his accident has left him unable to control his urination.

"No more than usual. Say doc, have I told you I'm a new grandfather?"

Out come the family pictures and so goes the rest of my visit with Johnny boy. I remind him on the way out how much I enjoy taking care of healthy people because it isn't much work. We both laugh.

"180/110, that's awfully high for your blood pressure."

I'm speaking to Paul Wilson, a patient of mine for many years, whose blood pressure is normally in good control. In his late forties, Paul works in a machine shop. He works hard and plays hard, is a bit overweight and probably drinks more beer than he is willing to admit to me or himself. Today he is in with his wife Kathy, also my patient. She usually does most of the talking.

"Is that bad?" she asks. "I've been so worried about him lately; he is always working so hard. I tell him he's got to slow down."

Paul just sits there and makes a sound resembling a grunt. He offers an unconvincing response,

"Maybe I ate too much salt."

"Oh no," says Kathy, "I'm very careful and don't use any salt."

I'm in an awkward position. Two months ago Paul called and asked if I could see a friend of his who didn't have any insurance and didn't have a doctor. I agreed. His "friend" was twenty years his junior; the two of them were having an affair. I wonder how this plays into the sudden loss of control in his blood pressure. I wonder how to address this in his visit today. Sure, I can increase his medication and probably improve control of his blood pressure, but does that address his health needs?

"Let's double up on your medication, and Paul, I want you to swing by tomorrow sometime so we can recheck your pressure. Maybe you can come by after work."

As I take the chart from the rack on the door, I inhale and exhale deeply. Anna Giaccomo is a tough patient. She's in her thirties, divorced, and suffers from a host of problems—headaches, body aches, fatigue, panic attacks—to name a few. She takes a lot of medications, but I don't see how to get her off any of them. We have tried counseling, pain clinic, and physical therapy, all without meaningful results. I am frustrated and I am sure she is too; yet, she keeps coming back, and I have not given up.

"Hello, doctor!" Usually she looks distraught, but today she is beaming.

"I have a surprise for you. I stopped all my medicines."

Needless to say, I am skeptical but I reply,

"Really, Anna, that's interesting! How do you feel?"

"I feel wonderful!"

She then explains to me that she went to a healing service. During the course of prayer she felt herself engulfed by a bright light. The light started at her head and moved through her body. She fell to the ground unconscious and when she awoke she had no pain. I just listen. I am both humbled and grateful that Anna is healed.

I am rounding in the hospital and stop to see Tara Robinson. This is a sad situation. She is only thirty five and has metastatic gastric carcinoma. She is unusually young to have this and it is very aggressive. In spite of all our medical interventions, chances are that she will die within a few months. We both know this. She is normally a quiet person and in truth I don't know her all that well. She is intelligent and attractive but has not revealed much to me about who she is. In spite of the gravity of her disease she has never complained or seemed too ruffled. I can only guess that the plans she may have made for her life had to be radically altered to contend with harsh realities. Nevertheless she never seems angry and seems to be at peace. This is the first time I am seeing her in the hospital. She is here for some chemotherapy.

"Good morning Tara, how are you feeling?"

"I was feeling nauseous, but they gave me some medicine and now it's a little better."

I marvel at her strength and at how well she is handling things. My eye is drawn to her bedside table where I notice a Holy Bible. The leather jacket and the pages are obviously well worn. Something clicks and I understand this young woman much better. I leave her room thinking, "She's going to be all right."

Justin Bernstein sits before me with a hopeful look in his eye. He is a relatively new patient of mine whom I am seeing again with complaints of fatigue. Justin is in his early twenties and is an avid runner, religiously running at least five miles per day. Enrolled in graduate school, he's working on a degree in organic chemistry. I hold him in high esteem as I particularly disliked organic chemistry. Justin is very health conscious, makes sure he gets plenty of sleep, and follows a vegetarian diet. He is a picture of physical fitness and has a completely normal physical exam.

"So what did my test results show, doctor?" He sounds hopeful.

"All your blood tests were normal." I reply. I can see the look of disappointment in his face.

"So you're saying there's nothing wrong with me?"

"It's good that your test results are normal. We were checking for a number of things some of which are potentially serious. Fortunately the tests were all negative. But clearly something is going on. If everything was fine, you should be feeling fine and probably wouldn't be in here to see me."

He nods. "Do you think I should take a vitamin?"

"It's perfectly fine if you want to take a vitamin, but they are not magic pills and I don't think they are the answer to your feeling better. There is a reason why you feel tired. We just haven't figured it out."

In my mind I am considering the possibilities. Justin's physical exam and lab tests are fine. He denies stress. Maybe he is worried that he's been exposed to AIDS and hasn't been able to verbalize that to me. Maybe I need to consider less common, more esoteric diseases that could explain fatigue. Perhaps he never wanted to go into organic chemistry and really wanted to be a musician, but parental pressures pushed him into his current studies. Maybe he is just working too hard and his body is trying to communicate that. I consider these and another half dozen possibilities.

"So, Justin, tell me what you like to do in your spare time."

"Well, there really isn't much extra time."

"Hmmm..." I think, maybe we're on to something.

Part One:
Integral–A Better View of Health

Photo courtesy Paul Schnaittacher

Chapter One:

Signposts-Markers that reveal your current location

How we define and conceptualize health is central to the foundation of this guidebook. Webster's New World Dictionary defines health as "soundness of body." Most often, people conceptualize health as the absence of disease. I believe each of these notions is inadequate in describing or understanding what we truly mean by health. What does it mean to be healthy? I just introduced you to Johnny Gerard who clearly has a significant physical disability which severely compromises the "soundness of (his) body." Yet, I do not view him as unhealthy. Indeed, I have portrayed him as he is—robust, full of vitality, and overall quite healthy. Contrast his physical state to Justin Bernstein whose body is quite sound; yet, I hesitate to label Justin as healthy. Tara Robinson's body is ravaged by an aggressive malignant disease, yet she seems to be in relatively good health. What is at play affecting the health of Mary Perkins and Paul Wilson? What changed in Anna Giacommo's body during that prayer service? Is there something we can measure or point to which explains how she crossed over from a state of poor health to good health in her moments of unconsciousness? With these poignant examples in mind, the notion of what health is seems much more complex.

When I had just started my postgraduate training and was an intern (the next step in medical training after finishing medical school,) the Chief of Medicine, a reputable cardiologist, challenged us with a hypothetical scenario. He asked us to consider two identical twin brothers who both suffered identical heart attacks at the same time. In this hypothetical scenario, both brothers suffered identical amounts of damage to the myocardium (the heart muscle). Six months later these identical twins follow up with their cardiologist. While they both have tests which reveal identical cardiac function, one of the brothers is judged to be healthy while the other remains quite ill. He asked that we consider this seeming paradox and I ask you to do the same. As an impressionable young doctor this story really stuck with me.

How an individual reacts to illness plays a huge role in their recovery. We can posit that one brother used his heart attack as an opportunity to examine his diet and exercise habits and work hard to improve them. Indeed, I have cared for many individuals whose health a year after suffering a heart attack is dramatically better than prior to their heart attack in spite of now having a damaged heart. Often, serious physical illness precipitates depression. The depression can persist long after the physical illness has been cured. Doctors sometimes refer to a "post cardiac syndrome" to describe this depression in heart attack patients. This could explain why one brother remained ill while his twin was well.

Illness and disease do not happen in a vacuum. They occur in unique individuals with unique home lives, family support structures and past experiences. Perhaps the twin who recovered had a loving and devoted wife and family who assisted his recovery. Perhaps the brother who remained ill had a best friend who died from a heart attack and he feared the same would soon happen to him; ultimately, this prevented his recovery. My Chief of Medicine never gave us an answer as to why one twin was healthy and his brother was not. In this hypothetical scenario the question has more significance than the answer. I have come to understand that for this particular set of twins there could be one answer but a completely different answer might explain the difference in another set of hypothetical twins. In some sense, these examples may seem to illustrate that "health" is rather mysterious.

But is it? Is health mysterious? Is it elusive? How is it that some people have it and others don't? How do we get it or get more of it? First we need to clarify what we mean by health. I've given some commonly held concepts about health and tried to illustrate why these notions are inadequate. Health goes beyond soundness of body or absence of disease. From my perspective as a practitioner of a healing profession, I have come to understand that each of us have a physical, a mental, and a spiritual dimension to our selves. Although it is appealing to segregate these into separate compartments, each of these components relates to the others. Each of these components integrates into a whole.

When there is a problem in one area it affects the other areas and affects the whole. The entire system has a dynamic quality with constant interplay among the various segments. Here I am describing **a system which is integrated and dynamic**. In this "health" model, **balance within the system determines the true measure of health**. What are your views about health? Consider that what you believe about your health is critical to how healthy you see yourself. How do you define being healthy for yourself? Give it some thought.

In my belief about health as I have begun to outline for you, a deficiency or excess in any of the three areas, body/mind/spirit, can cause the entire system to become unbalanced. The result—a state of impaired health. In order for you to chart a pathway to better health, it is crucial for you to understand that **deficiencies or excesses in one area can be compensated for by changes in the other areas. The key to health is net balance in the entire system**. Thus, Tara Robinson can enjoy good health in spite of her cancer. Her spiritual development compensates for her physical illness.

This is not a new concept, but somehow this concept has been lost in modern medical care. This model of health would be considered holistic. The integration of mind, body, and spirit into a dynamic balanced system represents what I believe health is all about. I particularly like to conceptualize this as harmony. Think of a symphony orchestra playing beautiful music. The components to consider are the music itself, the conductor, and the musicians with their instruments. When they are all working together at peak performance the result is magnificent. Harmony! What if one musician is not playing particularly well during a performance? Can the rest of the system compensate and still result in good music? If any of the components is impaired and there is no compensation, the result is an unbalanced system. The result is discord. This is analogous to being unhealthy or out of balance.

Let's expand this concept further. An orchestra can perform in a recording studio or in a recital hall. Does this affect the result? Absolutely! We sometimes say things like a performer "feeds" off the audience, or describe the audience as "flat". Some recital halls have excellent acoustics. I once had the privilege of attending a performance at La Scala in Milan. The sense of history and magic from just being in that hall elevated the performance. What am I saying here? Quite simply, we do not live in isolation. Our minds, bodies, and spirits are constantly interacting with the world around us. We are each a dynamic integrated system constantly interacting with a greater integrated system. That greater system is also dynamic and itself is in a lesser or greater state of balance and or harmony. When our internal physical, mental, and emotional components are in balance with a well-balanced external environment the result is a symphonic masterpiece— the sweet music of **Integral Health**!

Ken Wilber, a contemporary American philosopher, has described a framework for "Integral Medicine". In his model there are four different quadrants to consider as playing a role in an individual's health. A comprehensive discussion about his model surpasses the scope of this guidebook, but the simple principles are easy to understand. One quadrant relates to the body, one quadrant to the mind, one to our culture, and one to society. Obesity is not just a physical description of the body. Embedded in the label of "obesity" are associations that affect an individual's psyche as well as sociocultural judgments and labels. What we consider obese today was looked upon as healthy in the culture of the middle ages. Consider the acceptance of fast food and supersizing in our society, or media manipulation about the importance of being thin and you begin to see the role of social factors in obesity.

In Wilber's Integral approach we are asked to not focus on a single quadrant but to begin to see how all four quadrants have relationships to one another. To get a complete picture we must look at all four quadrants. A diet, which really focuses on the physical quadrant, is not necessarily the best solution to an individual's obesity. Emotional, social, and cultural factors need to be considered. Ask yourself, what does it really mean to a person's health to be diagnosed as HIV positive? How does this affect an individual's mind, mood, his/her relationships, likelihood of being fired from their job, etc.? What cultural and societal taboos and judgments are associated with this diagnosis—sexual promiscuity, homosexuality, and drug addiction? How is recognition of these circumstances brought to bear on the care of someone who is HIV positive? Does a combination of prescriptions address the true health care needs of this person? Can someone who is HIV positive enjoy good health?

Do you think recognition and appreciation for these integral concepts—how your mind, body, and spirit relate to social and cultural realities, are important in choosing a path to better health?

Think for a moment of the sense of enjoyment and pleasure you experience on a crisp autumn day walking through the woods. The fall foliage is resplendent, the sun is radiant, birds and rustling leaves assuage your senses. Contrast this with a walk in a crowded urban slum on a sweltering summer day. The air is stagnant, filled with exhaust fumes and you are assaulted by the blight of broken buildings, strewn garbage, and the press of humanity. In the first setting you are surrounded by the beauty of nature. Do you believe this is health enhancing? What about the second scenario? Just contemplating it gives me a sense of "dis-ease". Walking in this setting would not enhance my health. Imagine walking from the first to the second scene over the span of five minutes. What fundamentally has changed to the components of your own system? Very little. The system around you in the form of the environment has changed dramatically and this has an impact on your health.

This extreme hypothetical example illustrates a point; it demonstrates the importance of considering ourselves as a system within a system. **When there are excesses or deficiencies in the external system around us, we must adjust our own internal system in order to compensate and to maintain balance.** Sometimes we can make changes in the world around us that can improve our health. This could be as simple as straightening out a chaotic mess in our home. **Developing an awareness and understanding of the impact of what is happening all around us and how it affects our health is important in learning how to enhance our health.** With a more comprehensive understanding about health you can make more informed decisions and choices to help yourself enjoy better health. I hope you are now beginning to think about health in a different way.

We frequently do not appreciate the interactions among mind, body, and spirit and the role these interactions play in determining the state of our health. Often, we do not incorporate an appreciation of the role our surroundings play in affecting our health. The dynamic system comprised of our physical, mental, and spiritual selves is in dynamic interaction with the system comprised of our environment, our society, and the world at large. These are the signposts we need to begin to recognize and understand in order to move on a pathway to better health. I have not defined health but I have hopefully given you a different notion of what health is all about—harmony, balance, integration.

Each of these signposts marks a trail which you can follow to arrive at your destination. Trails are connections between locations. In a sense, you are at a certain location with respect to your health. Your goal, to move to a location of better health, requires that you follow a set of trails to get there. At the end of this guidebook, you will construct a map describing the territory of your health and chart your course along these trails—physical, mental, spiritual, and environmental. Each of these components has a role in determining your health and well-being. Let's begin our exploration of these four integral components.

Chapter Two
Body-Your means of transportation

In the *Wizard of Oz*, Dorothy's dog Toto pulls back the curtain exposing the "wizard". Let me play Toto for a moment and expose some features of Western medicine, the discipline with which I am most familiar. In trying to assess an individual's physical health it is important to understand the mechanisms of disease. Training in Western medicine, also referred to as "allopathic" medicine, relies on a disease model to diagnose illness. According to this model, diseases can be classified as resulting from a variety of causes. These include: congenital (i.e. present at birth, includes genetic), traumatic (from injury), infectious (secondary to germs), neoplastic (due to cancer), autoimmune (when the body's immune system attacks itself), metabolic (disruptions in normal biochemical regulation), vascular (pertaining to blood vessels), degenerative (cumulative damage over time). Typical examples of disease according to this classification scheme are as follows: cystic fibrosis—congenital; paraplegia secondary to injury—traumatic; pneumonia—infectious; Hodgkin's lymphoma—neoplastic; rheumatoid arthritis—autoimmune; diabetes—metabolic; stroke—vascular; osteoarthritis—degenerative. Essentially all forms of physical diseases can be placed in one of these categories.

Training in allopathic medicine primarily focuses on determining if a disease process is present (diagnosis) and the appropriate management of that disease process (treatment). The methods employed by the Western trained practitioner to reach a diagnosis include history, physical examination, and laboratory testing. At a much more basic level, I want you to consider health in terms of balance. The net result of some traumatic, metabolic, neoplastic, etc. process is to cause imbalance. At this moment I am purely focusing on the physical domain, but here I have made a very crucial distinction between physical health as defined by disease, contrasted to health as defined by balance. Disease is either present or absent. For the allopathic practitioner health is primarily characterized by the presence or absence disease; that's what their training focuses on determining. I prefer to consider health as a spectrum with wellness and illness at each end.

Considering health from a systems viewpoint, the presence or absence of disease tells us nothing about how well the system is in balance and essentially very little about the individual's overall health. Wellness, however, connotes balance and illness connotes imbalance. A systems approach demands looking beyond the single variable of physical problems. There are many good aspects to the conventional allopathic approach to diagnosing and treating disease, but the approach is inherently fragmented and focuses primarily on the physical domain. As such, the presence or absence of disease is used to determine how healthy a person is.

Have you ever been to the doctor when you do not feel well only to be told that you check out fine? Are you satisfied with your medical care? Recognizing some of the limitations of the conventional approach to care may help you understand your level of satisfaction. Part of the reason people seek non-conventional approaches to health care stems from the failure of conventional medicine to address them as complex individuals. **It's a whole lot easier to treat a disease than it is to treat a person.**

In the absence of a disease process, certain day to day activities can act to promote or to antagonize physical health. These activities relate to daily choices we make about such things as the foods we eat, how active we are, how much sleep we get, and what toxic exposures we encounter. Although no disease process might be at play when we choose to eat an "unhealthy" meal of fast food, we have at that moment done something which affects our physical health. While having a sedentary lifestyle in and of itself is not a disease, it provides a background that can lead to imbalance in our metabolism. Our bodies have a natural rhythm triggered by the day/night cycle and we all have a certain sleep requirement. Failing to appreciate and respect these normal body rhythms and cycles by having poor sleep habits can result in physical imbalance. Ultimately this affects our integral health.

When viewed in this manner, you can begin to understand that assessing physical health goes beyond identifying the presence or absence of disease. What is happening in the areas of nutrition, exercise, and sleep are basic and fundamental to assessing an individual's physical health **irrespective of whether or not a "disease" is present.** When a disease is present these areas are of even greater significance since the disease itself is associated with imbalance. Every effort should be made to enhance or restore balance in the physical body by focusing on the things we do which affect our physical state. Think of your body as your way of getting around, your means of transportation. Whether you are on foot, riding a pack mule, or driving a sports car, you are more likely to go further if you take good care of your body/mule/car. Who wants to break down on the side of the road?

If you want to avoid an unnecessary breakdown, the primary physical ways we can affect our bodies are to concentrate on our dietary choices, our exercise behaviors, and on our sleep habits. There are many very sound approaches which are readily available and give guidance in the areas of healthy dieting and healthy activity in the form of exercise. **Nutrition and exercise are day to day choices we make that have an impact on our physical state and are entirely within our control. These choices either act to enhance our physical health or to detract from our physical health by promoting imbalance.** The same is true of our sleep habits. Many adults simply do not get enough sleep; they suffer from sleep deprivation. This has a deleterious effect not only on their physical health but on their mental health as well. I cannot overemphasize the importance of respecting your body's need to get sufficient rest. Take a moment to reflect on some of the choices you made today. What food choices did you make? How active or sedentary have you chosen to be? How did you pay attention to your rest needs? What better choices can you make tomorrow?

Following a physical trail to improved health requires awareness and attention to proper nutrition, exercise, and rest. No matter what your current state of health is; no matter whether or not you suffer from a disease, you can improve your health by improving your diet, your type and level of exercise, and your sleep habits. In addition certain unhealthy habits such as smoking or excessive drinking act to imbalance our physical state. Eliminating or minimizing these unhealthy habits act to reduce this imbalance and improve health.

Chapter Three:
Mind-Pilot and navigator

Allow me to play Toto again (Toto is a nickname for Vittorio, my name in Italian and how my dear mother-in-law likes to address me) and pull back the curtain on the Western view of mental health and mental illness.

The allopathic approach to disorders of the mind uses a different format from the organizational structure used to understand disease processes affecting physical health. While the same physical processes might be at play, (e.g. a glioblastoma represents a neoplasm of the brain, Alzheimer's disease is a degenerative illness) the effect of these physical processes on things such as mood or cognition requires that mental disorders be classified very differently. In many cases of mental illness, we do not understand what physical processes underlie various mental states.

The Diagnostic and Statistical Manual of Mental Disorders (DSM) is the most widely used classification scheme. The current edition lists seventeen broad categories of disorders. Included among these categories are Schizophrenia and Other Psychotic Disorders (characterized by loss of reality contact), Mood Disorders (such as depression or manic-depressive disease), Anxiety Disorders (e.g. panic attacks or post-traumatic stress), Eating Disorders (such as anorexia nervosa), and Personality Disorders (e.g. antisocial). Here I have listed six of the seventeen categories and given some common examples. Using this classification scheme a doctor or mental health professional will try to determine if mental illness is present and translate this into a diagnosis. Various constellations of signs and symptoms and test result scores are all tabulated to determine if mental illness exists

Once again, a disease model is being used, although the classification scheme is quite different from that used to determine what type of physical disease is present.

The classification of physical disorders which I described in the previous chapter is based on different processes (traumatic, neoplastic, etc.). The *DSM* classification scheme is based on descriptions of different behaviors, thoughts, and moods. Since mental health entails much more than the presence or absence of disease, the *DSM* classification has limited value as it only catalogues mental disorders. Such an approach does little to characterize the entire spectrum of mental health —wellness on one end and illness on the other.

What are the qualities by which we measure and identify the workings of the mind? They entail such elements as intelligence, personality, thoughts, memory, emotions, and desires. All of these elements have a common basis in the anatomy and physiology of the brain and nervous system. Everything we think, everything we feel, whether real or imagined, correlates with some event affecting our anatomy and/or physiology. The incredibly complex networks of neural connections which are modulated by neurochemical signals ultimately are associated with thoughts and feelings. Stimulating a particular area of the brain can provoke memories, hallucinations, sexual arousal, etc. But our minds are more than the moment to moment state of neurochemical activation in our brains.

Our understanding of brain anatomy and physiology has advanced significantly since I majored in Neurobiology and Behavior in the mid 70's. This understanding has radically advanced the approach to treating certain types of mental illness. Thus, we now understand that depletion of the neurochemicals serotonin and norepinephrine is associated with a clinical state of depression. A drug such as *Prozac* helps to boost the brain's serotonin level which reduces the feelings of depression. St. John's Wort works the same way. This is a wonderful example of balance. A neurochemical imbalance has an associated behavioral affect, mental illness. Restoring balance improves health.

Rather than relying solely on descriptions of symptoms of depression such as sadness, fatigue, disrupted sleep, loss of libido, etc., we can use this example to illustrate a process underlying the clinical state of depression—reduced levels of the neurotransmitter serotonin. But there is a danger is trying to simplify all of the workings of the mind to a set of physical processes. Such an approach ultimately reduces the mind to a physical entity. (Philosophically, this is termed scientific reductionism a discussion of which is beyond this guidebook.) What you feel, what you believe, what you imagine, and what you experience cannot be described solely by physical alterations within your brain.

Although this example illustrates the point of illness resulting from imbalance, most of us are unable to measure the serotonin levels in our brains. For practical purposes, while it is easy to understand this concept of balance as being central to an individual's mental health, we need an easy way to assess mental health. A somewhat radical simplification comes from the arts. Philosophers and playwrights talk about reason and passion. These represent the workings of the rational and the emotional parts of our brains. The rational part of your brain is often associated with the higher level cognitive structures that first developed in mammals. The emotional centers evolved much earlier and are sometimes called the reptilian brain. Let us apply the notion of balance to these two areas. If there is balance in the "rational" part of your brain, you should be thinking clearly and appropriately. You would have no difficulty reasoning or with analyzing circumstances. Difficulty thinking and irrational thoughts would be indicative of imbalance. Happiness and positive feelings would suggest harmony in the "emotional" portion of the brain, while sadness and negative feelings might indicate imbalance. Where am I going with this? **If you could easily asses or evaluate your own mental health by examining certain thoughts and feelings, you could assist yourself in charting a pathway to better mental health.**

While we are familiar with evaluating such physical domains as diet, exercise, and sleep habits, most individuals are not accustomed to examining the domains of mental health. It is relatively easy to step on a scale and realize that you are overweight. We have a good tool to make that judgment—a scale. Most individuals lack the equipment to recognize persistent anger or unresolved grief or any of a number of other common problems which affect mental health. Recognizing that you are overweight you can then choose to diet and exercise to improve your health. The inability to recognize common thoughts and emotions which signal poor mental health make it difficult to follow with a choice to improve your health. The self-assessment chapters later in this book will assist you in evaluating the state of your mental health. If you are having trouble concentrating it might help to know that sometimes that happens when you are depressed. Anger and sadness both frequently occur with grief reactions. Addictions are often rooted in attempts to diminish a dysphoric mood or create a euphoric mood. With guidance, you can learn to read and interpret what you are experiencing with your thoughts and emotions and how this relates to your mental health. You can then consider your mental balance and see how this relates to your integral health.

My best friend's father is fond of saying, "People are all the same, they just have different heads." How profound! The thoughts and emotions, thinking and feeling, cognitive and emotive, rational and irrational, mammalian and reptilian parts of our minds are literally what's going on in our heads and what make us unique. They form the substance of who we are and ultimately act as the pilot and navigator that determine where we are going and what we are doing. What we think and what we feel drive our decision making to choose. Will I eat this or smoke this, reject this, study this, stay a while or leave? Do I choose to get married, stay with this job, get angry, feel sad, seek revenge, or go fishing? At some level life is merely a series of choices. **Reason and passion inform those choices**. Since you want to make good choices about your health, and you don't want to wander around lost in the territory of your health, I'll spend a good deal of time in sections that follow helping you figure out what actually is going on in that five pound appendage sitting on top of your shoulders.

Chapter Four:

Spirit-The driving force

What can we say about spiritual health? As I researched background for this book, I came across numerous references to research into prayer and health. Many of you are no doubt familiar with studies showing improved outcomes in ill patients who had other people praying for their recovery. Many of you may know of someone like Anna Giaccomo, the patient I introduced earlier who experienced spontaneous healing during a prayer service. Is this a miracle? How do we fit this third component, spirituality, into a framework similar to what I have described for physical and mental health?

In each of the two previous examples, I have given you models where we can consider balance or imbalance in a system component. Spirituality seems to differ so much according to different faiths and cultural traditions. We tend to broadly separate spirituality into "Eastern" and "Western". Perhaps you have explored different spiritual practices such as Zen Buddhism, Sufism, or Christian mysticism. What about New Age spirituality? Clearly human health cuts across all religious, spiritual, and cultural backgrounds. A Tibetan monk can be affected by diabetes or schizophrenia as well as a devout Jew. What are the commonalities in spiritual health?

I believe the answer to this is really quite simple. Most religions and spiritual belief systems have some reference to God, gods, a creator, or a supreme being of some sort. Let us simply call this a power greater than ourselves. Let us hypothesize that an individual can be somehow connected to this power to a lesser or greater extent. Spiritual practices such as prayer or contemplation strengthen this connection. Other behaviors can weaken this connection. While I am most familiar with Christian teaching in this area, all the great wisdom traditions of the East and the West share many commonalities at this fundamental level of spirituality. Christians strive to live in closer union with God. Sin distances them from God. American Indians refer to a Great Spirit; much of their spirituality has to do with nature. A desecration of nature disconnects them from this Great Spirit. In keeping with the holistic model for health which I have described, **this process of connection or disconnection to a higher consciousness determines the level of balance or imbalance in an individual's spiritual health. In the most simplistic way, more connection equates to more balance which equates to better health.**

In my experience as a primary care physician, I have noted that adults who strike me as being more spiritually connected seem to enjoy better health. Furthermore, when these individuals have to contend with some emotional stress or physical ailment, they generally seem to do better than individuals who lack this spiritual connection. What is the role of faith in God in health and disease?

Although we can readily accept parameters and principles which pertain to physical and mental health, many people seem reluctant to consider spiritual health in a similar way. Why is it so easy to consider mind and body aspects of health and ignore the soul? If we take a common medical problem, depression, and rename it as despair (a spiritual malady), how does this affect the management? In one instance management calls for efforts to improve mental health, the other points to a spiritual road or pathway to improved health. On many occasions I have felt the best medical advice I could give a patient was to return to church, speak to their minister, pray more, or somehow strengthen their spiritual connection.

But, the places in our lives where we grow, strengthen and nurture our souls go well beyond traditional religious outlets. In my own life, a quiet walk in the woods or time spent in my garden nourishes my spirit as well as time spent in prayer. In the same way we benefit from having tools to self-assess our bodies and our minds, we need tools to help us to better understand and evaluate our spiritual health. These same tools can help us to find those areas in our lives where we can cultivate and grow our spirit. **Essential in selecting and guiding you down a trail to better health is an appreciation of the**

spiritual dimension to your life and how it impacts on your overall health and well-being.

Allopathic medicine does not typically address this area of health. Nothing in my medical school training focused on this dimension of health. They don't teach how to take a spiritual history in medical school. There really are not any laboratory or diagnostic tests to order which reveal much about how ill or healthy an individual is spiritually or whether a disease of the spirit exists. Yet, in the holistic view of health I am asking you to consider, I believe the state of one's soul has much to do with a person's overall health. Once again, the concept of balance is appropriate. If you eat too much or you starve yourself, you will likely suffer adverse health effects. Failing to properly "feed" your spiritual self also results in poor health. Since we are all spiritual beings at our core, what is the effect of starving our soul? **The extent to which you are connected to a greater consciousness and the degree to which you are spiritually balanced have a huge impact on your health.** While this might sound mysterious and I cannot offer you physical proof, I can attest to the importance of the state of an individual's soul (however that is measured) and that individual's health.

In this discussion of spirituality, I think it is important to recognize that **religion and spirituality are not synonymous.** Religions provide organization and explanations about some aspects of spirituality; in many instances they provide guidance and structure to connecting with the infinite. Someone could easily be very religious but not be very spiritual. By the same token, someone else could be highly spiritual, but not very religious.

There are many opportunities to connect spiritually and to grow and nurture your soul that have little to do with organized religion. I have alluded to a quiet walk in the woods and to working in my garden as places where I am able to connect. The simple task of baking a loaf of bread—proofing the yeast, mixing flour and water, kneading the dough, and deeply inhaling the aroma of the baking bread, can be done in a way that nourishes the soul. I once grew wheat in my backyard, harvested and threshed the grain, ground the grain into flour, and then baked a loaf of bread. The kind of nourishment and sustenance this provided me cannot be matched by the bread typically purchased in the supermarket. That loaf of bread fed my soul! Just recounting the experience with you feeds my spirit.

Practicing "mindfulness" and having an awareness throughout the day of the presence of the divine can both be a path to spiritual fitness. Religious ceremonies, prayer, and contemplation are all ways to improve our spiritual health. How do you connect with the infinite? Do you feel spiritually balanced? People who are more spiritually connected often experience an expanded sense of consciousness. Along with this they feel more loving, more forgiving, and more compassionate. Is this a way you would like to feel? Do you recognize the role spirituality has in your health?

Unfortunately, many of us live spiritually malnourished. Our senses get bombarded daily with sights and sounds and sensory overload that all work to distance us from our spiritual centers. Our thoughts are consumed with future plans, tasks, past hurts, and our focus narrows to just getting through the day. We tend to be so scheduled from one moment to the next that we spend little or no time in between tasks. Quiet stillness provides some of the best opportunities to nurture our spirits. Even thousands of years ago, before fast cars, TV, cell phones, and microwave meals in a bag, mystics escaped to the desert to remove themselves from the distractions of their time in order to connect more deeply with the divine. How many more distractions do we contend with in our hyper paced modern times? We must learn to appreciate the time between tasks. Much as the time between notes defines the rhythm and "soul" of a piece of music; how we manage our time can create balance or imbalance in our spiritual lives.

Have you ever had moments of simple joy and connection to what seems to be infinite? At these moments, time seems to stop. There is no time at the source! **Most of us need to spend more time connecting to our spiritual centers. This exists at the very core of each and every one of us.** There is no need to starve your soul! Anyone can exercise and strengthen their spirituality. In fact, more often it is not so much effort to "exercise" your spirit as to sit back, loosen the spiritual blockage and let your soul shine forth. When you follow this path your health will improve. Is this a miracle? As my five year old nephew likes to say, "I don't know, you tell me."

Chapter Five:

Environment-The world you are traveling in

Thus far I have discussed three domains which impact any individual's health. These three components—mind, body, and spirit dynamically interplay in each and every one of us. Health or disease in each component part affects our overall health, and compensation in one area can offset deficiency in another area. In the holistic view I am advancing, harmony and balance among these domains represents a much truer and complete picture of one's health. Yet, we do not live in isolation. To get a truly complete picture of health, we also need to consider the environment in which each of us lives.

Here, I am using environment in a much broader context than is typically considered. Your surroundings are not just your physical environment—the quality of the air you breathe, the presence or absence of toxins or pollutants, the amount of germs or pathogens to which you are exposed, etc... Certainly your immediate physical environs, extending all the way to the biosphere, contain features which affect health and disease. But, **social factors and cultural factors are every bit as important**. These are represented in the two lower quadrants of Wilber's Integral Model. While social and cultural factors are external to you, they influence your internal state. Your socioeconomic standing and your cultural upbringing, the presence or absence of family and community support, the clubs you belong to, the people you work with, the country you live in, the government you live under, the traditions and values you grew up with, what school you attended, and so on, all of these contribute to your health.

This much broader view of environment is more than most health care professionals are trained to consider; although, not entirely. As a student I received training in public health which dealt with obvious topics such as good sanitation and widespread control of infectious disease. Medical journals and the lay press are replete with information about such things as bioterrorism, arsenic levels in the water, and the depletion of the ozone layer (which will increase our exposure to dangerous ionizing radiation and cause an increase in certain types of cancer.) Typically, these are the sorts of environmental factors that people think about when it comes to health, but they constitute only a small portion of what I am including under environment. This is changing. Recently, Western medical journals have begun to place a growing emphasis on cultural competence or awareness of cultural determinants that affect healthcare.

Some illustrations demonstrate my point. What good does a correct diagnosis and prescribed medication do for a woman who cannot afford the prescription or has to choose between feeding her family and filling the prescription? What about the medical needs of a man who is mentally ill and homeless—is a prescription for medication the solution to his health needs? If I arrange for a patient to have a diagnostic test but the patient has no car, there is no public transportation, and this person has no concerned friends or family, how does this impact on their health? How connected are you with the people in your community? Do you have a network of social support—people you can rely on? What is it like to grow up in poverty or to be the only black family in a racist neighborhood? How would it affect your health to live in a concentration camp? Or prison? Or under threat that the police officials could enter your home at any time?

In the aftermath of terrorist attacks on the World Trade Center people felt less safe and secure. This represented an attack on our society, on our culture. Our security felt threatened. People were afraid. Following this external event, stress related illness increased. Can you begin to appreciate how all these environmental factors affect health? Interestingly, there was also a reported increase in people attending church following the 9/11 attacks. Is this compensation a spiritual pathway undertaken en mass to restore balance to a sociocultural stressor? Considering this broad view of environment, what environmental factors do you see in your own life that might be affecting your health?

Government policy helps determine who is eligible for health insurance, food stamps, transportation subsidies, child care assistance, Meals on Wheels, etc. Where do you live? Is it a neighborhood infected with drugs, crime and street gangs, or is it in an affluent suburb? Is it urban or rural? Are there good schools in your neighborhood? Do you let your children play outside? After you begin to ask these questions, try to see how your answers impact on your psyche, your spirit, and ultimately on your health.

You can begin to appreciate how socioeconomic factors play a role in health. Let's consider some additional environmental influences. Did you know that working in surroundings that include natural day lighting results in increased productivity and reduced absenteeism? Sun exposure affects vitamin D levels. There are receptors in your brain and blood vessels that respond to vitamin D levels. Certainly you can appreciate that the quality of the air you breathe and the water you drink affects your health. Endocrine disruptors present in our environment have the potential to affect fetal development. These occur as a byproduct of plastic production. Plastics are ubiquitous, i.e. they are everywhere around us. Hormone and pesticide residues are in the food we eat. How does this affect us? Have you ever considered the level of noise exposure and the degree to which your immediate living and work space is cluttered as affecting how you feel? These are just a few of the environmental influences which play a role in disease. **Your environment has a huge impact on your health.**

Now I'll elaborate further on this rather expanded view of environment. Many cultural factors affect health. If I am treating someone's diabetes, it's important to know if their cultural dietary preferences are rice and beans vs. meat and potatoes. This awareness and recognition affects their treatment plan. Until recently, here in America, it was culturally taboo to have cancer. The word "cancer" was whispered in hushed tones. It just was not something you let other people know about. This has changed to the point that we now decorate ourselves with ribbons and bracelets promoting cancer cures and cancer survival.

I once cared for a Chinese immigrant and diagnosed a form of tuberculosis affecting the lymph nodes. Even though treatment completely cured him, he lost his job and was essentially culturally ostracized by his community. He had to travel to a different city in order to work. How do you think this affected him?

Our cultural upbringing in part determines our response to illness. Do we bear pain silently and stoically or do we broadcast our suffering to friends and relatives and maybe even strangers? Do you seek medical care from a doctor or a shaman? Would you be comfortable having a midwife deliver your baby? Do you believe in the healing power of crystals? Cultural background and influences set the language, the values, and many of the beliefs by which we organize our thoughts and ideas. These include our thoughts and ideas about health and illness. What cultural biases and influences shape your views about disease?

See the whole world around you as constituting an environment that affects your health. This includes your room, your house, your neighborhood and community; your city, state, and country. This includes your nationality, race, religious affiliation, family, and friends. All of these factors interplay in a vast dynamic system which constitutes the domain of our environment. In this milieu your individual physical, mental, and spiritual components interact. All four areas must be considered to get a truly holistic measure of health.

VIDEO LINK # 2 IN APPENDIX

Chapter Six:

Integral You-Seeing your health from this new vista

Imagine the following symbolic representation. In your mind's eye, visualize a fine sailboat coursing through the water. (My grateful acknowledgment to Dr. Charles Barnes, psychologist, minister, and gifted therapist for this representation.) You stand at the tiller. A brisk wind fills the billowing sails and the boat steadily moves forward with grace and power. It's a beautiful sight! But, if the sails were torn, or the boat was leaking or you couldn't hold the rudder, or if there were storms at sea—it might not be so pretty. Indeed, the boat could capsize. All the various components must work together in harmony, and they need to adjust to many different environments—heavy winds, light winds, choppy seas, and so on. Any imbalance left unattended would certainly impede performance and could result in disaster. So it is with the systems that steer your health. Think of your health from an integral perspective. The sailboat is your body, the pilot is your mind, wind and current are spirit, air and water are the environment. Are you sailing smoothly? Where are you headed?

For a few moments let's go back to revisit our hypothetical twins. You recall the identical twin brothers who suffered identical heart attacks yet six months later one is completely healthy and the other remains ill. Having now outlined the four domains of physical, mental, spiritual, and environmental let us reconsider the ill brother's situation. He has just returned from his cardiologist who has told him that his heart is better than ever and he has made a complete recovery. So why does he feel so lousy? Is it because he is unwilling to exercise and eat well? Or maybe he is sick and tired of eating fish and longs for a nice juicy steak but will not allow himself this "indulgence". This angers him! Is it because he hates his job, has conflict in his marriage, or is worried he will have another heart attack? Maybe he blames his work or his wife for causing his heart attack. Maybe his wife is afraid that having sexual relations will cause him to drop dead. Maybe she is no longer sexually fulfilled and is having an affair which he senses or suspects. Did his heart attack cause him to lose faith in God and stop going to church? Or is he so busy trying to eat well and sleep well that he no longer finds time to pray? Or is it that every time he eats the red meat he longs for he feels guilty? Did he change jobs in the meantime, move into a new house, suffer a cut in pay, stop cleaning the yard, give up coaching little league?

You begin to get the picture; however, the predicament of determining why he doesn't feel well, of why he is ill, is even more complex. What if some combination of the above underlies our patient's illness? Or perhaps a better question to ask is why his twin brother is in such good health. After all, they are genetically identical which could imply that they should be identical when it comes to health. Presumably they even share many sociocultural similarities. And, they received the same medical care. Why is one brother doing so well? Does he have a better marriage or more friends or more financial security? Does he meditate? Perhaps he lives on a nice country estate or all of the above.

Oh my! What's a brother to do to figure this all out? Is his cardiologist supposed to sort out all of this? Maybe all of the things causing his illness were present before this man's heart attack or perhaps they actually caused the heart attack. Or maybe some completely different problem is now present in which case the heart attack plays no role at all! The doctor is trained to treat disease and has recommended the appropriate treatment. Does the cardiologist have the training or the time to get to the bottom of why his patient does not feel well?

You can begin to appreciate the complexity of health and begin to understand why it is a lot easier to treat a disease or an organ than it is to treat a unique human being. Typically our infirmed twin continues to feel unwell. Perhaps he goes to see a psychologist who determines that his problems are not psychological. Or perhaps he sees a psychiatrist who gives him a prescription for an antidepressant. Or maybe our man sees an alternative health practitioner who determines that the problem is heavy metal toxicity which requires chelation therapy. He might go for some hands on therapeutic touch or get his energy field rebalanced with no apparent explanation as to what caused it to get unbalanced in the first place. Or he may simply go down to the local health food store and start one supplement after another until he finds the right one or combination that helps him to feel better. Is this the best we have to offer?

Okay, by now you see my point. **Health care is badly fragmented**. Practitioners focus too much on the trees without seeing the forest. We are all individually complex systems living in a complex environment. Focusing on single aspects of health, such as the presence or absence of heart disease, without appreciating the many other variables which are contributing is not likely going to result in an optimum outcome. Each practitioner brings his or her own training and experience which act as filters that distort, dilute, and reduce the patient's experience to some diagnosis or ailment or deficiency, etc. Such reductionism is dehumanizing.

A unique human being has more than a disease; they have a unique experience of illness. **The failure to recognize and care for a person's illness experience results in needless suffering**. The good news is that many fragmented efforts to improve health which are directed in only one domain will actually affect the other domains and will likely have some beneficial effect. You can compensate for disease in one area by enhancing other areas. Remember there is a dynamic equilibrium among the component parts of the systems. Since health equates to optimum integration, balance, and harmony among all system components, an integral approach offers the possibility of treating the whole person. By correctly identifying problems in all the domains which affect health—physical, mental, spiritual, and environmental, an integral practitioner can recommend area the most comprehensive approach to improving health.

Having outlined this theoretical framework which holistically approaches health, the focus of the remainder of the book is to give you tools to begin to asses each domain. Indeed, you probably have begun to do so based on the types of questions I have raised. I will also outline some of the common traditional and alternative approaches to health and healing and explain in part why they are helpful. But first, we need to visit some important individual topics. Think of these as important landscape features with which you need to become familiar. Your ability to recognize and understand these features will have a marked impact on what pathway you choose to better your health and how easy your journey might be.

Each journey begins with a single step. Your first steps will take you inside your own head to explore what's inside. Bring a flashlight; it's pretty dark in there!

Part Two:
Hidden Areas to Explore

Photo courtesy Paul Schnaittacher

Chapter Seven:

Motivation-What pushes and pulls you along

Let's begin by thinking about motivation. Much of what we accomplish in life and, more often than not, what we do not accomplish, can be traced back to motivation. We have some nice common expressions that capture this—"Where there is a will there is a way." Alternatively, "Wishes don't wash dishes."

We all have many goals in our lives, and often many wants or desires. These may be pretty straightforward like a new car, or tickets to an event, or a desire to visit some exotic destination. Frequently these goals are somewhat vaguer such as a better marriage, or more job satisfaction, or more quality time with our children. Whether or not we meet these goals, how successful we are in achieving these desired ends, and how much time and effort is required is often determined by how well motivated we are. Do you get discouraged by having goals and not meeting them? How can you avoid this kind of discouragement? I can guess by the fact that you are reading this book, you likely have a desire to improve your health. Let's examine how this topic of motivation can assist you in meeting this goal to be healthier.

Imagine yourself in a rowboat in the middle of a lake. You see a spot on the shore where you would like to land. Your ability to get to that landing spot is primarily determined by how well you row your boat, how much effort you put into each stroke, and how long you continue to row. That's what motivation is all about; it's like rowing and sometimes towing your boat. When motivation fails, you essentially stop rowing. This greatly reduces your chance of successfully reaching your destination. Such a motivation failure makes achieving your goal unlikely.

Why do people stop rowing? There are lots of different reasons. For you, in your own life, the important question to ask is **why do you sometimes stop rowing?** Frequently, people are unrealistic in their expectations. They don't fully appreciate how much time and effort might be required to achieve their goal. We live in a fast paced society and often want instant results that don't require a lot of time or effort on our part. So, instead of a disciplined program of regular exercise to lose weight, we want to take a magic pill that will enable us to lose weight. Often, people start with a lot of motivation, but when the desired result isn't reached right away they begin to feel discouraged and their motivation sputters. This is much like grabbing the oars with lots of energy and enthusiasm and rowing with great strength at first, but then tiring out and giving up long before you have put ashore. **Failures in motivation thus can be secondary to being unrealistic in what is required for resources (time and effort in this example) and failure to persevere**. Perseverance is a quality of stick-to-itiveness. It's the, "Slow and steady wins the race" approach that served the tortoise so well in the popular children's tale about the tortoise and the hare. Think about times in your life when your inability to persevere compromised how well you achieved your goals.

What motivates people? Lots of different things motivate different people. Some individuals have a strong desire to succeed, some people like power, or money, or nice possessions. Some people are motivated to please others, or do things for the people they love. We all have basic needs which we are motivated to meet. These include things like food and shelter. Then there are higher order needs such as to love and be loved, or to be accepted among our peers, or to be respected by our children or coworkers. The failure of these needs to be satisfied often provides a strong source for motivation. In much the same way as when you are hungry that motivates you to find food, when you are "hungry" for some higher order need such as love, this motivates you to fill your need.

In our lives we sometimes confuse needs and wants, but both of these can be powerful sources of motivation. Guilt is a strong motivator. It can sometimes be the driving force behind positive behavioral changes. Fear is another powerful motivator. Although I do not ordinarily advocate relying on either guilt or fear as the primary motivators in an individual's life, I have seen many people use these very effectively. For instance a smoker who suffers a heart attack may feel guilty about having smoked and this might motivate him or her to stop smoking. An episode of chest pain might scare someone into losing weight for fear of having a heart attack. In truth, **any strong emotion can power motivation**. Love, anger, hatred are all powerful motivators. Examine your own life for a moment and consider when your success in achieving some goal was essentially driven by underlying emotion.

I would now like to focus particularly on health and where motivation plays a key role. I have already asked you to conceptualize health in relation to four different domains— mind, body, spirit, and environment. Let's consider examples from each area. Imagine that you are feeling a lot of stress and would like to devote more time to some stress relieving hobby. Or perhaps you are overweight and would like to slim down to improve your health. Maybe you have decided that you would like to pray more. Or you may want to improve your home environment particularly your relationships with your children by spending more time together. Any of these examples could conceivably improve your health. All of these examples require behavioral change. Effectively changing behavior is often related to a combination of negative and positive reinforcers. **Understanding positive and negative reinforces in your life can literally be life changing**. Generally these can be external or internal. In the examples above, feeling less stressed because you are spending more time with an enjoyable hobby is a positive internal reinforcer. Having your spouse upset at you because you are stressed all the time is a negative external reinforcer. Stepping on the scale and seeing your weight down is a positive internal reinforcer. Being unable to fit into your favorite jeans is a negative internal reinforcer; while having your coworkers comment on how great you look is a very positive external reinforcer. I can go on but you begin to see the point.

Here is a crucial point to develop awareness about. **Both positive and negative reinforcers affect motivation**. There is a saying that, "Nothing succeeds like success." In general, being successful at accomplishing some task helps to sustain motivation; it is a positive reinforcer. Not being successful, a negative reinforcer, can sometimes boost motivation as in we redouble our efforts or focus on trying harder. In this way it is helping to motivate. **Often, negative reinforcement leads to discouragement which poisons our motivation**. When you are contemplating some personal effort to improve your health it is helpful not only to examine your motivations but also to think about what positive and negative reinforcers, both internal and external, might affect your effort. This might sound like a lot of work, but it becomes pretty easy once you do it a few times.

Let me illustrate with a very common situation in clinical medicine, a patient who wants to stop smoking. A good place to start is to ask, "Why do you want to stop smoking?" This zeros in on motivation. Let's suppose the reasons given are the following:

1. I get out of breath easily and want to feel I can breathe better.
2. Cigarettes have gotten so expensive I can't afford them.
3. I want to be there for my children.

Here you see the first reason can be put in the context of internal reinforcement; having difficulty breathing is a negative internal reinforcer, while breathing more easily is a positive internal reinforcer. Using this information can result in a plan that asks the patient to remind themselves every time they feel out of breath why they are trying to stop smoking. Or, we can instruct the patient to measure how far they can walk before getting out of breath and then ask them to repeat this two weeks after they are no longer smoking. If they can walk significantly further it provides a positive internal reinforcer to help sustain their motivation.

The second reason can be used to set up internal or external reinforcers. Money saved by not smoking can be used by the patient to treat themselves, a positive internal reward, or to treat their spouse, a positive external reinforcer. Or a negative reinforcer can be used effectively such as asking the patient to set aside an additional $5.00 every time they buy a pack of cigarettes (negative internal) or asking their spouse to specifically complain about the waste of money every time the patient smokes (negative external).

Continuing this analysis, the third reason cited can be used to assist motivation. The patient can be instructed to attach a picture of his/her children to their package of cigarettes and look at it when they take out the pack. If looking at the picture results in not smoking it has worked as a positive internal reinforcer, while it can act as a negative internal reinforcer if the person winds up smoking. The children themselves can externally provide positive or negative reinforcement by expressing gratitude when the patient does not smoke or concern when they do.

The same type of reasoning can be used in examining why the person smokes (i.e. what is reinforcing the smoking behavior?) and crafting a strategy for behavioral change. If, for example, smoking is pleasurable for this individual (a positive internal reinforcer) we can ask the person to pair an unpleasant visualization with smoking, e.g. imagine your lungs filling up with soot (a negative internal reinforcer). I urge you to spend time examining what internal and external reinforcers and rewards are at play in your own life.

Think about what behavioral changes you would like to accomplish, your motivations for adopting this new behavior, and what internal and external reinforcers can be used to help you to sustain your motivation. Think also about why you persist in your current behavior, what motivates you to continue to do something you really want to change, and what reinforces your continued behavior. Are you the type of person who needs your family cheering for you on the shoreline in order for you to row your boat (respond well to external reinforcement)? Or are you the kind of person who would like to row to shore but drifting along suits you almost just as well (poor internal reinforcement)? What's it going to take to get you to row all the way until you get there? I am sure there are things about your health that you would like to change/improve. **Until you ask yourself these sorts of questions and develop a strategy using reinforcers, you might suffer a motivational block that impedes your success.**

Although there are other places in this book I offer the following advice, nowhere do these words ring more true. **In your efforts to positively accomplish healthy behavioral change you are your own worst enemy. The flip side of this is that you are also your own best ally.** Whose team are you playing for? You can nurture your motivation or you can squash it. The choice is yours to make.

Here is some more food for thought regarding motivation—understand that motivation fluctuates. Some days you may be highly motivated, other days not so much. These fluctuations in motivation are perfectly normal. It is sometimes worthwhile to have a special plan to deal with moments of weakness, times when your motivation fails. This is a plan or strategy to develop in advance as it is very difficult to resist temptation at moments of weakness. If you are trying to stop smoking and are faced with a strong urge to smoke, maybe your plan could be to call your best friend on the phone and ask for a pep talk. (Hopefully you have solicited your friend's support on this before calling them at one o'clock in the morning!) Maybe your plan can be to walk around the block. Even highly motivated individuals, with the best of intentions, have moments when they just lose their willpower. **Having a plan to deal with these moments can be the difference between accomplishing and not accomplishing your goals.** Think for a moment about some healthy behavioral change which you have attempted but not achieved due to a failure of willpower at a moment of weakness. Do you think having a strategy to get through the weak moment could be the difference between success and failure?

As a quick summary, learn to think about motivation in terms of rowing your boat. Ask yourself what's keeping you out in the middle of the lake and why you should or should not row yourself to some point on the shore where you have decided you want to be. What needs and what wants are at play? What emotions are involved? What strategies have you used in the past as successful motivators? Understand what internal and external positive and negative reinforcers are relevant that can boost your motivation or demotivate you. Are you disciplined to persevere in your efforts to sustain your motivation? Work out a strategy to deal with moments when your motivation weakens. Be realistic.

Chapter Eight:

Addictions-Digging a deeper hole trying to get out

Suspend for a few moments all your preexisting notions about addictions. It is our inclination to distill and characterize addictions as ___(blank)___ person is addicted to ___ _(blank)___ thing. This is not very helpful. It's looking at the end result without understanding the causal relationship, the underlying process. Addictions develop in an effort to remove ourselves from an undesirable current state and take us to a place where we somehow feel better. **Addictions occur as we attempt to recreate these inner states where we feel better.** Past experiences associated with a particular state provide the template for addictions.

The most common addictions people often call to mind are usually associated with the individual's desire to recreate a sense of **euphoria.** Euphoric states are pleasurable in some manner to the individual. They can be **activating** as in a heightened sense of power or strength or clarity of mind or enhanced sensation. This is what people who are addicted to cocaine are trying to achieve. Or these states can be **deactivating** as in feeling very relaxed or mellow or "chilled-out" as people may experience who are addicted to drugs such as Valium. More often, addictions are not an attempt to induce euphoria so much as to counteract a **dysphoric** state. Dysphoric states are unpleasant in some way to the individual. Dysphoric states can result from too much activation as may occur with feeling anxious or stressed or "pissed-off". Alternatively, dysphoric states can accompany times of deactivation such as feeling sad, or "bummed," or feeling like your brain is fogged, or you don't have any energy. These highs and lows are common experiences and are not the way most of us like to feel.

We have lots of ways to alter these dysphoric states which we have learned from past experiences help to change the way we feel. Caffeine can sharpen our mind and give us an energy boost. Tobacco can mellow out some feelings of stress. So can alcohol. **Any activity or substance that we crave in order to induce euphoria or counteract dysphoria can become an addiction.**

You might be surprised to consider some of the many addictions in our society. I'm sure you are familiar with some of the common addictions such as drugs, alcohol, tobacco, gambling and sex. Some of the other addictions are less commonly recognized because they are more socially acceptable; they can include such things as exercise, work, or shopping. Our modern society provides us with new sorts of technological addictions such as TV, video games, web surfing, and internet chat rooms. I once had a patient who was spending about 10 hours per day playing an on-line multiplayer fantasy game. This was a serious addiction for this man, but fortunately he was able to recognize this and give up the game. Consider violence as potentially addictive. It has the capability of altering dysphoria and for some people inducing euphoria. Thrill seeking is a common and often under recognized addiction for some people. Are you a workaholic? A shopaholic? Do you regularly use activities or substances to induce euphoria or to combat dysphoria?

Our brains are truly remarkable. The neural pathways or neural nets which excite certain parts of our brain arise in response to various stimuli. A built in memory of the excitatory and inhibitory pathways can become hard wired into our neural circuitry. If we like the way we feel when these circuits are activated we naturally want to activate them frequently. There is a strong reward system wired into our brains to repeat the steps that activate these circuits which result in our somehow feeling better. This is the state of neural activation which we want to recreate because it helps us to feel better. If chocolate recreates that state, then you will crave chocolate. If it's sexual excitement, then that's what you will seek. If being the center of attention is what makes you feel better, then you will seek to be the center of attention. Whatever activity or activities that you have learned will provide the right stimulus to activate the neural circuits will be the activity or activities you seek. **This paired stimulus and response essentially leads to the cycle of addiction.**

So how do we break this cycle? **There are three different variables upon which we can act in order to break the addiction cycle.** First is the **underlying state** (e.g. the underlying dysphoria). Second is the **stimulus** and third is the **response.** Helping you to learn to recognize your internal state will be covered in some of the self-assessment tools later in this guidebook. Once you are better able to asses and to examine your own physical, mental, emotional, and spiritual state you will understand yourself better. This better self-understanding will empower you to take steps to change in ways that will replace an underlying unhealthy state with one that is more healthful.

Addictions are like a huge roadside billboard telling us that something unhealthy is present. Addictions indicate a state of imbalance. The addiction itself is not the problem. In many respects it is the solution to an underlying problem. But, it is an unhealthy solution which itself causes problems. In this sense, it is much like finding yourself in a hole, but your attempts to dig yourself out only make the hole deeper. **Addictions are the wrong approach to restoring balance.** When your underlying state is healthy, you feel well; consequently, there is little motivation to alter this good feeling. If you are in a good place, why would you want to change that? If you are not feeling well, there are healthy ways of restoring balance—the subject of this entire guide. These healthy ways to restore balance provide better alternatives to addictions. Choosing a healthy alternative is the way to get out of the hole you find yourself in instead of digging yourself in deeper.

The second variable in the addiction cycle, the stimulus, is the substance (drugs, tobacco, food, etc.) or the action (shopping, gambling, video gaming, etc.) that activates those parts of the brain which recreate the desired state. So, any efforts to reduce or eliminate access to the stimulus can help to break the cycle. For example, throwing away the cigarettes, not buying any chocolate, getting rid of the credit cards, or setting time limits on TV viewing are all things which people can do to reduce addictions.

Response represents the final variable in the addiction cycle. Response is often the most difficult to change. Generally this involves using some other stimulus which alters or supersedes the pleasurable response. The prescription medication *Antabuse* is used to help in alcoholism. When someone who is taking this medication consumes alcohol they get a very unpleasant sick feeling. As a result, the same stimulus (alcohol) which used to produce a favorable response (feeling mellow), now causes an undesirable response (feeling intensely nauseous). Since addictions often result in adverse personal or social consequences, these consequences can sometimes provide the stimulus to break the addiction.

When you focus only on the result, an addiction, instead of on underlying causal chain which underlies the addiction, it is very difficult to break the addiction cycle. It's much more productive to think of addictions as solutions (albeit poor solutions) to particular problems. Examining the state which an individual seeks to change, the stimulus, and the response represents a method to understand addictions and to develop healthy solutions to the underlying problems which the addiction is attempting to solve.

Many people feel victimized by their own addictions. They feel controlled by the addiction and unable to break free. Think in your own life what behaviors constitute addictions. What underlying factors are at play? Do you believe that a life free of addictions is healthier? With guidance, understanding and motivation you can break the chains of whatever addictions you have.

Chapter Nine:

Relationships-Rules of the Road

Probably the most important feature to examine on this journey to better health is to notice what is going on in your relationships. Indeed, after our basic survival needs have been met, relationships are probably the major element which determine the quality of our lives and in some respects our happiness. Here I am talking not only of the quality of our relationships with others, but also where we stand in relationship to ourselves and the world around us. You, as a unique individual, are in relationship to your family, friends, coworkers, and community. Furthermore, you stand in relationship with your career, your values and ideals, your hopes and aspirations. It is important to step back and examine where you stand in these relationships and how this impacts on your health.

Balance and harmony are key concepts to consider in examining these relationships. Indeed, as has been discussed in many parts of this guidebook, imbalance and discord underlie illness and poor health. Unfortunately, most of the professional examination of relationships and health falls in the arena of mental health counselors and psychologists. Since many people are averse to going for counseling, they do not get the benefit of professional guidance to help address conflict in relationship and poor quality relationships. Good, healthy relationships are like healthy nutrition. Are you well-nourished or starved?

Let's start out by looking at how we relate to other people around us. I would first ask you to consider the significant other people in your life—your spouse or significant other, parents, children, friends, and loved ones. Are there aspects to your dealings with these others which cause you pain? Do you sometimes feel disappointed or angry or frustrated by the actions or behaviors of these others? Are you sometimes wondering why they did something or perhaps didn't do something? Do you feel let down or "pissed off"? Do the actions or non-actions of these significant others cause you to feel hurt or confused? I do not know a single person who does not occasionally or frequently experience these negative thoughts or feelings. What is going on here?

In many respects we each have a set of rules which govern our relationships. **These rules determine how we and the people we relate to are supposed to act**. Some of these rules are stated, such as, "Do unto others as you would have others do unto you." Most of the rules are unstated. So, if I do you a favor, I expect you to return the favor, even though neither of us has stated this as a rule. **The "rules of behavior in our relationship" may be almost entirely unstated.** Unfortunately, my rulebook may not be the same as yours. If I violate one of your rules, or you break one of my rules, then one of us is likely to be confused or disappointed as somehow our expectation has not been met. How we react to this failure of expectation is likely negative—anger, frustration, hurt, etc. You can see how **failure to meet one another's expectations frequently is at the root of conflict in relationship. Embedded in this is a failure to communicate. But frequently, we are not even aware ourselves of the extensive set of rules and regulations which we have in our own rulebook.**

The failure to communicate is not necessarily an intentional withholding of information, a refusal to share what guides our mutual expectations around how we relate to each other. Rather, we have never fully explored or even read our own set of guidelines and therefore we cannot share them with someone else. Often it is trial and error with lots of stumbling along the way until we figure out what rules govern our relationships. If we are successful, we can enjoy good relationships. Frequently we are unsuccessful or only partly successful. As a result, our relationships are fraught with strife. It is not enough to say that poor quality relationships are a result of poor communication when we ourselves are often not aware of what we need to communicate to the significant people that we relate to. **You can't communicate what you yourself do not understand.**

A superb example of this is very well articulated by Gary Chapman in his excellent book, "*The Five Love Languages*". In summary, he explains that people communicate love in five basic but different ways. Each of us has a primary love language that we speak. If your way of saying, "I love you!" is by doing helpful things, but your partner's way is through spoken words, "I love you, I cherish you, I appreciate you…" you are speaking different love languages. Thus, if your partner is showing love by doing all sorts of nice things for you but not speaking the words of love you need to hear, you may not be feeling loved. Similarly, you can be telling your partner how much you love them, but if you aren't backing it up with loving actions by what you are doing for them, they might not feel much loved at all. It isn't that you don't love one another; it's just that you are speaking different love languages. No surprise here that there may be some hurt, confusion, tension in your love relationship.

This is just an illustration that what is written in your rulebook about "rules governing love relationships" is different from what is written in your partner's guidebook about how to demonstrate love. Absolutely, there is a failure of communication between you, but neither of you is even aware that you each have a different set of expectations. Eventually, through trial and error you might figure it out, but for the moment one of you is speaking Martian and the other Venusian.

A subtext of many of our rules for relationships detail **what you think you should be giving into and what you should be getting out of this relationship**. Essentially all relationships involve some sort of exchange. But it isn't like a market exchange for goods or services. It isn't like paying twenty dollars in exchange for a shirt or five dollars for a car wash. Our mutual understanding about these types of commercial exchanges are relatively clear cut and there are various laws which stipulate what expectations go along with these types of transactions. In relationships, often what you are giving are such things as time, energy, emotional investment, and personal sacrifice. What you get in return are things like companionship, support, camaraderie, love, security. **It's difficult or impossible to ascertain what constitutes a fair exchange in these sorts of interpersonal relationships.** In particular, when you consider that my need for security or emotional support and what satisfies those needs may be very different than yours, you can begin to appreciate how complex interpersonal relationships can be.

So where do all these unstated rules and regulations which govern relationships come from? Where are your expectations about giving and receiving in relationships derived from? **Many, many factors influence what goes into your rulebook**. Modeling from your parents, cultural factors, ethnic influences and your values all play a huge role. Media exposure through television, movies, internet, books, magazines, and newsprint all play a role. Classroom learning, observing others around you, social etiquette all contribute. So does your life experience, particularly as you are growing up, and especially what your experiences have been in prior relationships. Essentially, **these things act as internal programming**. All of these are important factors which influence what you expect from another person. Truth is, no two people have the same set of rules so it's no surprise at all that there is a tremendous amount of dysfunction in interpersonal relationships. And it should come as no surprise that two people trying to have a conflict free relationship requires a lot of work and understanding, especially if they come from different cultural, ethnic, socioeconomic or life experience backgrounds. A lot of differing expectations need to be worked through.

Let's bring this home with some real life examples. You are feeling upset with your friend because you left a message on her home answering machine two days ago and she still has not returned your call. Not only are you disappointed but you are wondering about the strength of your friendship. A couple of weeks ago you had a message on your home machine from this same friend and you called her back the very same day. Well, what you don't realize is that your expectation—return call within 24 hours, is different from your friend's—return call within 4-5 days. You each have a different set of rules which governs this piece of your relationship. Unfortunately, this friend has now violated one of your rules. Consequently, you feel hurt while your friend can't figure out why you are now giving her the cold shoulder—she thought you were friends. Oops!

Your parents were strict disciplinarians and you were raised to be quiet and respectful and do as you're told. Your spouse was raised in a very laid back home with only a few restrictions. You love one another dearly but can't seem to agree on any aspects of child rearing and you can't understand why your children aren't more like you when you were growing up. No surprise here; you both have very different guidelines regarding raising a family.

You go out with your spouse every Friday night. Friday afternoon you get an unexpected call from an old friend who is passing through town and wants to have dinner. When your spouse gets home you left a note saying you went out with this friend. When you get back, your spouse is really angry at you. This reaction totally surprises you as you didn't anticipate anger; in fact, you thought your spouse would have enjoyed having some time alone. What happened? Your rulebook indeed states that you acted totally within reason— unexpected visit from old friend trumps usual Friday night out with spouse. Your spouse's guidebook reads a little differently—plans are plans and you don't change a prior commitment without discussion; a note is totally unacceptable. You never even realized that this would create a problem. Instead of stepping back and examining why this conflict occurred (different sets of guidelines) you get into a fight about who is right and who is wrong. Naturally, we want to defend our position. Sometimes it's hard to hear or understand someone else's position, but this creates a whole new secondary set of relationship problems.

When we fail to recognize and acknowledge the different sets of rules which govern our relationship expectations, we tend to want to defend our position and/ or attack the other person's position. The result is battle lines are drawn and there is a fight. The fight could be one person trying to dominate the other with their set of rules or it could be one person withdrawing into a defensive position by refusing to change. It's a lose-lose situation for the relationship. In one case, one person feels controlled by the other and there is no conflict resolution. In the other case, a wall or barrier isolates one individual from the other and there is no conflict resolution. Sometimes both people are on the attack, trying to win the battle. Other times both people withdraw to a defensive position with what is essentially a demilitarized zone separating a standoff.. Often this "truce" follows repeated but failed attempts to attack the other's position. But **a truce is not a resolution and these barriers become difficult to deconstruct**. In some respects, people manage to walk themselves into a veritable quagmire. Meanwhile, the person they might need to depend on the most to help get them out is mired in their own muck. Yikes, it's a mess! But with time and effort you can make your way back to solid ground.

Sadly, many people are effectively at war in most of their relationships. They may not realize it but they are doing battle with their children—usually trying to control them, with their family and spouse—frequently a mixture of attacking and defending the positions in their rulebook, with friends and with coworkers. Is this healthy? Being in constant battle mode in your relationships is not only fatiguing, it seriously diminishes your well-being.

How well balanced are your relationships? Take a look at some of the significant relationships in your life and focus on where you feel upset, or frustrated, or hurt, or angry, or disappointed, or fed up. Ask yourself which of your "rules of behavior" have been violated. Try to figure out what the person you are in conflict with might have written in their rulebook. Explore where you have engaged into battle mode in your relationships. With whom are you in the attack mode and with who have you withdrawn into a defensive position? With whom and on what issues have you adopted a truce? Can you let go of some of your rules? Can you work to reprogram some of the relationship guidelines you now have? Are you willing to reflect on why you are having trouble in your relationships? Do you think by understanding some of your internal programming you can better communicate your relationship needs and wants to your significant others? Do you think that tension and conflict in relationships will simply go away on its own? Recognize that **having healthy relationships requires effort**. But also realize that having healthy relationships is so beneficial to your own health and well-being. Learning to read and recognize the "rules of the road" that govern relationships will enable you to get around faster, smarter, and with a whole lot less pain and suffering.

By no means do I want to oversimplify what is a very complex topic. While having healthy relationships is key to your own health, **not all relationships are healthy**. If violence characterizes one of your relationships, if physical or emotional abuse is part of your relationship with someone else—either as giver or receiver, take courage and **seek professional guidance**. Many difficult relationship problems are truly beyond the average person's ability to correct or repair. The terrain here can be very rocky and dangerous. If you have gone through the self-examination I have guided you through and feel you cannot fix a serious problem, be honest with yourself and get help. There are many resources available to help you.

Beyond your relationships with other people, you are also in relationship with your community. This includes your neighborhood, apartment complex, nation, and the world. What is written in your rulebook about these relationships? What is your subtext about what you should be giving and what you should be receiving in the context of these relationships? Are your expectations being met? Do you begin to see how your health is affected by the quality of these relationships? If crime and litter are part of your neighborhood have you withdrawn into a defensive position to try and insulate yourself? Would you be willing to try and change your neighborhood by participating in a street watch or organizing a cleanup? Are you involved in your community; how do you view yourself as a member of your community? Can you contribute in some way to make it a better place? Do you think volunteering in your community will help you feel better about yourself and to make your community better? Responsibility is part of relationships. What is your responsibility as a global citizen? How do you approach improving your relationships with the world around you? Are you unhappy, angry, frustrated, or disheartened because your expectations about the world around you are not fulfilled? Are you somehow constantly struggling with or battling against these disappointments from failed expectations? How does your reaction affect those around you? Think about what you can do to improve these relationships.

Thus far I have focused on how you relate to others and the world at large. In the integral model these represent the association between you as an individual and to the collective you live in. That collective makes up much of the environment you live in. But there are a whole other set of relationships you have with yourself as an individual. Are you, for instance satisfied with how you stand in relationship to your career? Undoubtedly, you have an internal set of guidelines about what you should be giving and what you should be getting out of your career. Are you in balance with this relationship? Perhaps your career is taking too much of your time and energy. Or, perhaps your career has gone stale and is no longer fulfilling. Take a moment and consider your relationship with your work. Are feelings of anger, frustration or disappointment which you experience somehow rooted in internal rules or expectations about your work which are not being met? Is your work a source of enjoyment and satisfaction in your life?

Think about where you stand in relationship to your values and ideals. Have you made compromises which leave you feeling a little unsettled? **Integrity is a measure of how closely we follow the values we hold**. We all have a set of underlying personal guidelines and expectations which govern how we conduct ourselves. Are you meeting your own expectations about yourself? If you are, you undoubtedly feel harmonious about your relationship to yourself. If, on the other hand, you are not meeting your own expectations about yourself you will experience discord. How you react to this could explain why you feel unhappy (about yourself), or angry (at yourself), or down (on yourself).

If you are out of balance with yourself, spend some time reviewing your self programming. Are your rules governing your relationship with yourself unrealistic? Let's face it, nobody's perfect! But if your rulebook says you have to be perfect or best or first all the time, you have set yourself up for disappointment. Remember where all those rules came from. They are a product of many different influences such as parents, teachers, society, and religion. **Don't be afraid to examine your internal programming.** It's very healthy to do so. You may discover that some of the entries in your rulebook are outdated or ridiculous or unhealthy. It may be time to update or rewrite some of those rules. If you are out of alignment in your relationship to yourself, make this the first relationship you work on improving. If you are taking a misaligned, out of balance self into relationship with others you are starting from a point of imbalance. **Working on your own internal relationship with yourself can often be the best means of improving your relationships with others.**

Finally, I ask you to consider one other important relationship. Where do you stand in your relationship to Source? How do you conceive of God and where do you fit into creation? Do you believe in a God of justice, of mercy, of forgiveness? Do you see yourself as being on good terms with the Creator or are you at odds? Are you self-centered or God centered? Are you angry at God; do you feel abandoned by God? Do you feel connected to Source or disconnected? Spirit imbues all four quadrants of the Wilber model. **You are in relationship to Spirit at many different levels of connectedness**. How do you rate the quality of those connections? What spiritual beliefs do you have and how do these beliefs play a role in how you feel about the quality of your Spiritual relationship? Is this an area that needs improvement? How can you nourish this important relationship and help it to thrive?

Chapter Ten:

Forgiveness-An inner oasis where wounds are healed

"What you did really hurt me!"

"I am so offended by what she said!"

"I'll never speak to him again!"

Sound familiar? How about—

"I'm so sorry I let you down!"

"I wish I hadn't been so hard on her!"

"Maybe I was out of line when I yelled at him!"

It only seems right to discuss this next feature in the landscape of our lives following the section on relationships. Because **it is in the context of relationships that forgiveness is sought, is given, is withheld, and is received**. Why is it so difficult to say the words, "Will you forgive me?" And why is it sometimes so very difficult to respond, "I forgive you." Having said these words, does forgiveness truly represent how we feel inside?

If I could change one and only one thing about our educational system, I would include mandatory coursework and training in forgiveness. Too much pain and suffering is rooted in the failure to forgive. Let's face it, people hurt one another—this is a universal human experience. At times we have all been on the receiving end of that hurt. So too, we have all been on the giving side of hurting someone else. Who among us has not, at some time in their life been a victim of circumstance? With no one to blame for our pain and suffering can we still forgive or do we carry forth a grudge against the cruelty of our life?

Transgression, betrayal, injustice—life can be very harsh at times and life can be very unfair. **Because these and other painful experiences color all of our lives, there is a universal need for forgiveness. Forgiveness is the means through which our wounds can be healed**. Time alone does not heal the wounds of human transgression. Revenge does not make you whole. When we experience anger, misery and pain because we have been wronged, we remain in a state of imbalance. Failure to forgive keeps us mired in conflict and is bad for our health. Forgiveness rebalances us and helps to restore our health. Forgiveness represents an inner oasis to heal the wounds of transgression.

Let's take as a starting point some life experiences which could require forgiveness:

- Driving home from work you are rudely cut off by another driver.
- You show up to meet a friend and get stood up.
- Your partner is unfaithful.
- As a child you were sexually abused.
- Your child is killed by a drunk driver.

The normal emotional response to life events such as these includes things like anger, distrust, sadness. It is normal to react in these ways. Often, these life events become part of our life story. It may be recounted to a couple of people as in the case of being cut off while driving. Or it may continue for many years and be recounted and relived time and again. Over time, the emotional content attached to these episodes can evolve into something poisonous. Anger turns into resentment or persistent rage or a lifetime devoted to getting even. An episode of betrayal leads to a lifetime of distrust or a grudge that won't be let go. Sadness turns into bitterness or despair or apathy. **Sometimes the pain and suffering from these toxic emotional responses far outweigh the hurt from the initial transgression**. Sometimes, what develops is an endless cycle of transgression, followed by retribution, followed by transgression, and so on. It's tragic!

If the solution to preventing all this human misery is forgiveness, why do people fail to forgive? For some people, the fact that they have been wronged gives them some secondary gain such as support from others. By holding on to the hurt, they can play the role of the victim and we are all supposed to feel sorry for the victim. Sometimes a person's self-image is bolstered because they suffered from some wrong. In some strange way this becomes a badge or medal that supports their ego self. For some, not forgiving somehow vindicates who they are and gives them the excuse to be angry or bitter or untrusting or miserable. Sometimes it's pride that gets in the way. Some people equate forgiveness with weakness and we don't want to be perceived by ourselves or others as weak. Do any of these explanations account for times you have failed to forgive?

Often, people don't forgive simply because they don't know how. It isn't even mentioned in their rulebook about life. When they look in their book about what to do when life deals you a serious blow, forgiveness isn't even mentioned as an option. Sadly, most of our teachers, our role models, our leaders, and our society simply do not reinforce forgiveness. The Biblical Old Testament law of, "An eye for an eye..."—vengeance not forgiveness, still predominates. The New Testament teaching of, "Love your enemies..." hasn't caught on very well.

So how do you forgive? First, recognize that **forgiveness is a choice**. It is a choice about how you react to a grievance which has befallen you. The hurt, the transgression, the wrong which has occurred is an event. Forgiveness is one possible response that you can choose in how you react to that event. It is a decision you make.

Part of forgiveness is to acknowledge that a wrong has occurred. Remember, people hurt one another; this is a universal human experience. Life is sometimes unfair. Failing to acknowledge the wrong, the unfairness, the hurt is a form of denial. It's dishonest. But after you have processed the event and you have experienced pain you must next decide whether to hold on to your pain and all the emotional attachments that accompany it (the anger, sadness, etc.) As long as you hold on to the pain, and remember over time those emotional attachments tend to become toxic poisons, you have not chosen forgiveness. **Forgiveness occurs in the process of dissociating the event causing pain from the negative emotional attachments connected to that pain.** In the process of forgiving, you are letting go, you are releasing. The past episode remains as a past event. The pain which followed remains as a past response. But **the suffering tied to this event/response moves from present to past in the moment of forgiveness**. The result is that you can revisit the past hurtful event, acknowledge that there is pain attached to the event, but you do not continue to experience the emotional suffering in the present moment which that event caused. You have forgiven!

Dr. Fred Luskin, upon whose work much of this section is derived, heads the Stamford Forgiveness Project. His research has demonstrated some of the physical and emotional benefits of forgiveness. He correctly points out that some key elements about forgiveness are often misunderstood. **Forgiveness does not require reconciliation**. If someone has wronged you or hurt you, you can still forgive them without choosing to continue a relationship with that individual. This is important to recognize. By forgiving someone, it does not mean that you condone their action. Condoning or excusing their action would imply that it was okay. But it was not okay. It was wrong and it hurt.

Forgiving the person who wronged you does not imply that you accept their behavior as okay. Forgiving does not require forgetting. Indeed, you should remember painful events in your life. This is part of learning and forgetting sets you up for a repeat performance. Another crucial point to understand is that **forgiveness does not require the offender to ask for your forgiveness**. The decision to forgive is your choice. The decision to ask for forgiveness is some other person's choice. If you are waiting for the other person to beg you to forgive them, you are putting the power of forgiveness in someone else's hands. And, you are denying yourself the potential health benefits of forgiveness by making it contingent on someone else's behavior.

Thus far I have been discussing what it is like to be on the receiving end of transgression and the giving end of forgiveness. Sometimes the table is turned. Is it helpful to seek forgiveness from those you have grieved? When you have hurt someone else, and your relationship with that person is out of balance, you can restore balance to the relationship by obtaining their forgiveness. Understand that there is no guarantee that your apology will be accepted. You cannot insist that someone you have transgressed must make the choice to forgive you. That decision remains up to them. It doesn't hurt to try. Both you and the other person stand to benefit. If you are having trouble asking someone else to forgive you, ask yourself why.

For many people, forgiving others is much easier than forgiving themselves. As I discussed in the previous section, we all have a relationship with ourselves. When you let yourself down, that constitutes an event. If that event leads to feelings of anger or disappointment directed towards yourself, you have the choice to hold on to those feelings or to release them to the past and forgive yourself. Guilt and remorse are the sorts of emotional toxins directed towards ourselves that can be very destructive. These can result from failing to forgive ourselves. **Since we all fall short of the mark from time to time, we have lots of opportunity to practice self-forgiveness.**

Take a few moments and think about the difference between a hurtful action and how you reacted. Are you still carrying hurts that you have not been able to let go? Have these become poisonous to your psyche or spirit? Do you use these past events to blame someone or something for what's wrong in your life? Are you willing to make the health choice to forgive? If not, what is holding you back? Have you done things in the past that continue to trouble you? Are you in need of self forgiveness? Alexander Pope put it so well when he said, "To err is human, to forgive divine." Are you ready to embrace your own divinity?

Chapter Eleven:

Grief-Roots and ruts that trip you up

Thus far, as your guide, I have tried to open your eyes to features about health and disease which you may have overlooked. When you begin to recognize these previously overlooked features of your own health and wellness, the landscape begins to change and perhaps you see things differently. The landscape features haven't changed, just your perception of them. Hopefully, as you view your own health and consider these new perspectives, you have also begun to make connections between thoughts, emotions, physical feelings, and your state of well-being. Grief represents an important aspect to your health that you could easily pass by, but is sure to trip you up. Therefore, it's important not to overlook grief when you think about your own health.

Have you ever walked along a forest path only to trip on some twisted roots or some hidden rut? Grief is like those roots and ruts. It is present at many places along your journey. If you are attentive, you will see grief as a root in your path. At times when you stumble, uncovering that hidden rut may reveal grief underneath. To achieve your goal of better health, you need to learn how to spot, uncover, and confront grief. Sadly, this area of our lives is seldom explored during typical medical encounters. **In truth, it is grief's commonness that allows it to camouflage and blend in so well in our day to day lives**. Right now, at this moment, you are experiencing grief. My job, at this moment, is to teach you to spot it.

So what is grief? Quite simply, **grief is how we respond to loss.** Since life is a series of losses, we all must contend with grief. You are probably thinking about major losses in your life such as the death of a loved one—parent, friend, pet, and so on. Customarily, we think of grief in the context of death. But have you considered other losses in your life? Loss of our youth, innocence, physical health and abilities are things we all have to deal with. Do you miss the summer? Do you miss your old neighborhood or the house you grew up in? Do you miss an old friend or relationship that used to bring you joy but has since faded into memory? Have you taken on responsibilities and yearn for a time when you felt freer? Do you miss a time when your children were younger, or still lived with you, or a time when you were younger and still lived at home? Do you miss feeling safe and secure? Do you yearn for a time in your life when things seemed less complicated; or a time in your life when you had a better relationship with your spouse, or your children, or your siblings? Do you miss feeling well, happy, or full of energy?

Change is an essential fact of life and we must all continuously adapt to change. As such, we continually have to respond to loss. **We grieve!** Spend a few moments considering some recent and distant losses in your life. How do you think this has influenced your health?

How we grieve affects all aspects of who we are physically, mentally, emotionally, and spiritually. In this sense, grief is very holistic. Fatigue, insomnia, body aches and pains, changes in appetite, and a weakened immune system are just a few examples of physical responses which may accompany grief. Difficulty concentrating, confusion, loss of memory, or trouble thinking are examples of mental imbalance which may result from grieving some loss.

The emotional characteristics of grief have received the most attention, particularly as a result of Elisabeth Kubler-Ross. Many readers may be familiar with her groundbreaking research into grief and her details about the stages of dying: denial, anger, bargaining, depression, and acceptance. Her work provides tremendous insight into many of the emotional components relating to grief. How each of us grieve is unique and individual, but typically we experience a jumble of emotions. We may react to loss by crying, feeling irritable, or sad, or depressed. Anger, fear, anxiety and guilt are other emotional responses frequently tied to grief. These may all occur simultaneously.

At our spiritual core, responding to loss may generate anger towards God, or feeling abandoned by God. We may react by losing faith, feeling hopeless, feeling disconnected or deeply troubled as we search for meaning in the face of our loss.

Grief affects us at all levels of our bodies, minds and spirits. **Because all disease and illness involves change and therefore loss, wrapped up in almost any disease or illness lays a component of grief**. These sometimes hidden features of grief can manifest in many different ways. A man with coronary artery disease misses a nice juicy steak and doesn't understand why he feels angry. A woman with diabetes has some sweets for dessert, feels guilty, and doesn't enjoy her night out. An athlete with chronic back pain gets depressed thinking about all the things he can no longer do. A musician with crippling arthritis loses her sense of purpose in life and becomes gravely ill.

Sickness and disease can change our self-esteem such that we lose that feeling of, "I can do anything!" Faced with the losses that illness carries, we may grow bitter, resentful, or self-pitying. We may become timid, withdrawn, needy, or dependent. Learning to recognize these unhealthy responses is important. Confronting loss, we could just as well decide to be creative, or resourceful, or more determined. Ultimately, how we respond to loss is a personal issue. How do you respond?

There is a special form of grief which I want to call your attention to. While grief typically involves loss, **anticipatory grief** involves a response to a loss which has not yet happened. For instance, you may start grieving the loss of a loved one who is dying from cancer even though they have not yet passed away. You may anticipate losing something which you value and react to this expected or imagined loss even though it has not yet occurred. You may be feeling a sense of dread about something bad you anticipate may happen. Attached to this anticipatory grief may be all the physical, mental, emotional, and spiritual signs and symptoms previously discussed. **When you recognize imbalance in your life, whether it arises in your body, mind, spirit, or environment, learn to take inventory of your losses**. Remember to include anticipatory grief.

Although grief is a personal matter, from an integral perspective, culture and society play a part in your own individual grief response. What were your early childhood experiences with loss? Were you taught to stoically not cry or show emotion when someone died? Were you instructed to wear black clothes for a year and not to have any celebrations? Were you allowed to express your feelings and work through your grief? What beliefs and values do you have when it comes to remembering and honoring the dead? Do you party at wakes and funerals? Do you visit the graves of loved ones who have passed on? While death remains the chief event we associate with grief, **our culture, society, and relationships have much to do with shaping our response to loss and therefore our health in contending with loss**. How long is it "acceptable" to grieve when your last child moves out of the house? How long is it "acceptable" to mourn the loss of a job? Who mourns with you? When do others stop supporting your grief and giving comfort? When do others expect you to "get over" your loss? Does your job allow you a three day "bereavement" leave? Is this enough to mourn your loss?

Some losses are not validated by society or may have stigmas attached by culture or society which interfere with normal grieving. Not everyone views the death of a pet or breakup in a relationship as serious. How do you grieve learning that your brother has AIDS when the rest of your family does not know or will not acknowledge this? How do you mourn the death of a soldier friend in a war that you don't support? In a war that you do support? How is it different to mourn a murder victim than a suicide victim or death from an accidental drug overdose? How does it feel to grieve alone?

As I mentioned in the preface, "I don't have the answers to your health problems, but I do have the questions." These are the sorts of questions I want you to ask yourself. Examine grief in your own life from an integral perspective. You may be surprised to learn what you uncover. One thing I do know about grief from my own personal experience—it hurts! **Pain and suffering come along with many of the losses we must contend with**. Grief is a universal human experience. **Contending with grief takes energy**. Healing restores energy. The hurt that accompanies loss, the wounds that accompany grief can be healed.

In this chapter I have encouraged you to develop self-understanding about your own personal losses and your own way of grieving. Taking inventory of your grief will be covered in the self-assessment section. Your knowledge and understanding of your own grief will help you to avoid getting tripped up and help you get to a place of healing.

When I struggle with significant loss, I recall the words of Albert Camus, "In the depth of winter, I finally learned that within me there lay an invincible summer."

Chapter Twelve:

Destructive Emotions-Excess baggage that weighs you down

The palette of human emotion is rich in color and texture. The full spectrum of emotional expression runs from joy, bliss, and ecstasy to sadness, despondency, and abject despair; from exhilaration to funk to rage. Many shades temper the in between states of these highs and lows. But, bottom line, in a loosely organized and simplistic way, **we have positive, neutral, and negative emotional states**. As we view this vast emotional landscape, I would like to focus primarily on negative emotions as these are the ones which tend to be destructive in ways which reduce our health and well-being. Conversely, learning to cultivate positive emotions, those which help to restore balance, health, and vitality will also be discussed. Narrowing this further, we shall explore particularly **anger** and **fear** in the context of health. These two emotions stand out as major contributors to imbalance. They act as excess baggage that weighs us down and impedes our progress to reaching a place of better health.

Anger and fear both result in many of the same detrimental health consequences, but they tend to arise from different sets of thoughts and responses. **The common effect is a state of arousal**. Linked to this state of arousal are physiologic responses which result in the release of "stress" hormones such as cortisol. The emotional centers of our brain are linked to the activation (or deactivation) of our endocrine system, our autonomic nervous system, and our immune system. Scientific investigational tools such as PET scans, EEGs, and functional MRI scans allow us to see where are brains activate in association with different emotions. The over activation of these systems contributes to fatigue, heart attacks, strokes, and a host of other ailments. Often anger or fear are appropriate responses to what is occurring around us. Consider for instance the reaction of anger to witnessing a child being taunted by a bully, or recollecting being raped, or considering torture or slavery. All these could very appropriately generate anger. Consider also being chased by a rabid dog, or being lost in the woods, or experiencing crushing pain in your chest. Any of these would likely generate fear, a very appropriate response.

Anger and fear are not in and of themselves destructive emotions when they occur in the context of events such as described above. **They become destructive to your health when they occur with frequent regularity, exaggerated intensity, protracted over an excessive duration, or in circumstances and events where they are not appropriate**. It's curious that these same four variables: frequency, intensity, duration, and associated circumstances are the same variables we consider when assessing a medical symptom such as pain—e.g. how often does it occur, how strong is the pain, how long does it last, when does it occur/what makes it better or worse? In many respects, it is helpful to look at anger and fear the same way. Sometimes pain is not indicative of disease—I touched a hot stove, got burned and it hurt. But consider feeling the same burning pain in the absence of a provoking stimulation—perhaps this indicates a disease. Now consider anger that lasts all day because you got into a traffic jam that morning. Imagine feeling afraid every day that something bad might happen to you or your loved ones? These are symptoms of illness. They are landscape features in the territory of your health which you can not only learn to recognize, **you can actually change them**. Think of it as draining a swamp or clearing a pathway.

The expression "making mountains out of mole hills" comes to mind. How often have you taken a small fairly trivial matter (a mole hill) and built it into a mountain of anger? How often have you "worried yourself sick" over something that wasn't really a big deal? Think of times you have done this. Perhaps you can think of something that happened today as an example. When you begin to look at things that get you mad and keep you mad and things that cause you worry and anxiety you may discover you are not as healthy as you would like to be. Next, you might have the stark realization that you dug the swamp that needs to be drained and you placed the boulder in your path that you now need to clear. Wouldn't it be great not to have all this extra work cleaning up the mess?

To make this easy, let's first take a look at where anger and fear arise. **Both arise in the present moment, but in general, anger is rooted in the past while fear is typically rooted in the future**. There are situations where anger arises in anticipation of some negative future event e.g. you experience anger contemplating that your boss will deny your vacation request. This anticipatory anger is similar to anticipatory grief which was previously discussed. Most often, anger experienced in the present moment that is the source of unhealthy imbalance results from past events contaminating the present moment. Common examples include: you carry your anger about the traffic jam this morning throughout the day, you remain angry about a relationship that soured years ago, you do not let go of anger over some previous hurt.

We have many words to describe different forms and expressions of anger—annoyance, fury, rage, pissed off, peeved, incensed are just a few. Almost always, anger is secondary to something else—frustration, disappointment, a hurtful situation, loss, interference, someone else's anger. Let's illustrate—you are frustrated when your co-worker repeatedly dumps some unfinished work on your desk and you feel pissed off; you expected to receive some thanks or words of appreciation for doing your friend a favor and feel annoyed that no thanks were expressed; you are hurt when you find out someone you confided in has spread your confidential information to others and you feel outraged; your son or daughter is molested by his/her coach and you feel furious; you are in a rush to finish your shopping and your child needs to use the bathroom and you feel peeved; your boy/girlfriend is angry and starts to yell at you for something trivial and you react with anger. We all experience anger, which in and of itself is not necessarily bad or inappropriate. **It's unhealthy when we persevere with our anger, or continue to call it from the past to the present where it becomes corrosive, or make it too often our response pattern to the many frustrations, disappointments, and hurts that we all must contend with in our lives.**

In truth, when it comes to anger, we have a choice; actually, we have two alternative choices which can have a huge impact on our health and well-being. We can choose not to get angry in the first place when circumstances don't go our way, or we can choose not to overreact or to hold on to our anger so that it contaminates a large part of our waking lives. It's okay to get angry under appropriate circumstances, but there is a tremendous amount of judgment into what constitutes appropriate. **This judgment comes from your internal rulebook about life** which I discussed in the section on relationships. That rulebook is derived from beliefs, culture, society, previous experiences, role models, and a host of other influences. Take some time to think about times when you have gotten angry and what rules or expectations have been violated.

Can you rewrite some of those rules? Think about what triggers or provocative acts cause you to get angry. Are you following an "emotional script" which directs you to get angry when those triggers occur? Can you see yourself responding in other more healthful ways? There are two other aspects to anger which I ask you to think about as well. **Anger is often a precursor to aggression and violence**. Is a path of aggression and/or violence one you would choose to step onto? Wouldn't it be better to avoid that path all together? **Anger typically begets anger i.e. it's contagious**. Often there is escalation of anger as it passes to and from and among people. In this sense it's like a contagious disease leading to an epidemic. Laughter is also contagious; which would you rather spread?

While anger usually disrupts our present by taking something from the past, **fear always comes from the future to disrupt our present. When you feel afraid it's because you fear something bad is going to happen**. Worry and anxiety are two of the most common expressions of fear which we all have experienced. Fear is one of the ways we respond to perceived threat or potential harm to ourselves or something/someone we value. There is undeniable survival benefit in responding appropriately to potential harm. In the section on stress management I shall discuss the fight or flight response. In this sense, fear helps to arouse us physically so we can best respond to threat and maximize survival. To the extent that fear does this it is health enhancing; anything more is, quite simply, detrimental to our health. As noted earlier, **exaggerated intensity, excessive frequency or duration, or fear when no threat is present are all maladaptive**.

But there are so many things to be afraid of! It's easy to see the world as a scary place. On a daily basis we have to contend with insecurity rooted in job, finances, relationships, self-esteem. We worry that we or those we love may be the victim of violence or harm. Some of us live with fears of embarrassment, shame, social acceptance, and a host of other possibilities. We suffer from anxiety about the air we breathe, the germs around us, the possibility of flood or natural disaster or terrorist bombs. There's no shortage of things to be fearful about.

Anxiety is pervasive in our society and is part of our lives. To what avail? When you think about it, worry is largely a wasted human endeavor. **Worrying about something does not affect the outcome**. The "bad" thing either will or will not happen regardless of whether or not you worry. This is not to say you shouldn't be preparing for a possible hurricane if you live in an area where hurricanes occur. And this does not mean that you shouldn't secure your valuables when walking in a high crime district. There is a difference between taking appropriate precautions—a rational non-emotional response to maximize survival, and being overridden with worry and anxiety—an irrational emotional response that does nothing to maximize survival. When your fears of possible adverse future occurrences contaminate your present it becomes unbalanced and unhealthy. Once again, you are making a choice to allow this fear to disrupt your present. Why do you do this?

Anger and fear represent destructive emotional responses when they are either inappropriate or excessive. There exists a relationship among emotion, moods, and temperament. Emotions describe a short term state of mind and body activation; mood describes more of prolonged emotional state, while temperament becomes our baseline to describe our emotional state. These short and more prolonged feelings of emotion and mood correlate with activation in certain portions of our brain and nervous system and with the temporary and sustained release of hormones and neuroregulatory substances. **Over time, the circuitry of our brains adapt to our chronic emotional state**. As a result our brains can literally become mired in madness or wired to worry. Fortunately, the circuits can be rewired.

Think of some of the words we use to describe a person's temperament which is their nature or disposition—relaxed, care free, easy going, upbeat, somber, high strung, morose, sullen, nervous. What kind of people do you enjoy being around? What word would you use to describe your temperament? How do others characterize your disposition? What percentage of your daily time do you spend dwelling on past negative emotions and what percentage of your day are you thinking about negative future possibilities? How do you think this affects your health?

This section has primarily reviewed anger and fear as examples of destructive emotions, but there are other negative emotions—hatred, guilt, jealousy, and shame. So too, there are many positive emotions—joy, compassion, reverence, tranquility, equanimity, to name a few. According to Buddhism: "Emotions become destructive the moment they disrupt the minds equilibrium." *(Destructive Emotions How Can We Overcome Them? By Daniel Goleman)* Our scientific tools of investigation when used to examine the brains of advanced meditators such as Tibetan monks yield fascinating results. In the sense of balance, destructive emotions accentuate imbalance while constructive emotions restore and improve balance. By consciously directing their minds, the monks are able to activate or deactivate different parts of the brain which correspond to different emotional states. This is something we can all learn to develop.

Ask yourself honestly what percentage of your day you are choosing to be nurturing negative emotions and what percentage of your time do you nurture positive emotions? Ask yourself what things and circumstances in your life provoke anger and what generates fear? Why are you angry? Why are you afraid? Does this help you to feel healthy? Is this how you want to feel? You can unload the unnecessary and unwanted baggage of anger and fear.

I enjoy gardening. To be a successful gardener requires proper cultivation, watering and feeding. I like to think of destructive emotions as weeds. With continued cultivation, watering, and nurturing you can grow a whole mess of weeds. When you practice tolerance, patience, compassion, love and rejoicing you counteract the negative emotions and cultivate a beautiful and productive garden filled with wonderful fruits, vegetables, herbs and flowers, and few weeds. What kind of a garden do you want to harvest from? The choice is yours.

VIDEO LINK #3 IN APPENDIX

Chapter Thirteen:

Attitudes/Perspectives-What you see when you look around

Everything that we think and feel about health is, in some sense, in our heads. At some level, how we view our own health is wrapped up in our view of reality. How is this shaped? How is it formed? Can we reshape and/or reform our view of our own health? Allow me to digress for a few moments in order to give you a conceptual framework about how you develop your view of the world around you. Imagine a video camera set in the woods. It records the sights and the sounds around it. Let us postulate that a pack of wolves crosses in front of the video camera. What is recorded? Quite simply the video camera records colors, shapes, and sounds. The video camera cannot discern what this visual and audio input represents or its significance.

If we were to attach a computer to this video camera, we could program the computer to perform image and sound pattern recognition so as to correctly identify the pack of wolves. This programming would enable the computer to compare certain visual input patterns and audio input sounds with a stored data base in order to correctly identify the wolves. The video camera by itself is unable to do this function because it lacks analytic capability. The video camera is capable of only recording certain data but it cannot analyze the data. The analysis is performed by the computer based on its programming, i.e. its software.

If we happened to be standing next to this video camera we could not only record the visual and audio data and analyze it correctly to recognize the wolves, but we also would react to the information and respond. Our reaction would likely be fear and our response would likely be to try and run away to safety. Thus, **the chain of events described becomes perception, followed by analysis, then interpretation, followed by reaction and response.**

The first three steps are subject to error, the second two steps are subject to choice. Thus, if I were to place a filter or block on the video camera, it would perceive the world around it in a distorted way (perceptual error). If the computer had a programming glitch, the analysis of the data input could be flawed (analytical error). Interpretation is subject to…interpretation! How you react and respond to the information around you depends on choice. In the case of the wolves, you could choose to remain calm and to stay put, but getting scared and running away has a greater likelihood of survival and thus is a better choice. Making the best choice depends on accurate perception and correct analysis. Both are subject to error.

Our brains are designed for pattern recognition. This involves selectively ignoring certain perceptual input and processing the relevant details to make sense out of what we see and hear and touch and smell. Biologically, we are programmed for survival. As a result, we are programmed to recognize and respond to threat. Optimum survival depends on getting it right. Why is all this important when it comes to health? Quite simply, misperception, incorrect analysis, and misinterpretation frequently lead to unhealthy reactions and responses.

If we want to maximize our survival, we need to correctly perceive, analyze and interpret the world around us in order to make the best choices about how to react and respond. Your organs of perception gather the sights, sounds, tactile input, tastes, and smells around you. They function like a much more sophisticated video camera in the preceding example. Your brain is the organ of analysis and interpretation functioning as the computer hardware while your mind functions as the software. Your mind is making sense of all this perceptual input to determine what your reaction/response is.

All this happens in real time for events happening at this moment. But, we are capable of bypassing the perceptual input step and, using our imagination, we can create an entire scenario totally within our minds which we then react and respond to. We can imagine a pack of wolves in our mind's eye which leads to a reaction/response. Such a chain of events can also lead to healthy or unhealthy choices. Optimum survival here also depends on making the best choice, but in this case, it's in response to a totally imagined event. In response to imaginary events we all frequently make poor choices, unhealthy choices. These choices promote illness rather than wellness and do not support optimum survival. Often these reactions and responses happening in the present moment are derived from analysis and reanalysis of past events and circumstances. Often our reactivity is in response to imagined future events or circumstances, things which have not even occurred and perhaps never will. Like I said, we live in our heads!

Allow me to illustrate these concepts with a few real life examples. You notice blood on the toilet tissue after going to the bathroom (perception). Your analysis— this is nothing serious and you do not seek medical care. Or, your analysis is that this is very serious and your reaction is fear that you have cancer. You observe that your coworker did not greet you when you passed each other in the hallway (perception). You conclude (analysis then interpretation) that he does not like you which leads you to feel angry and unhappy all day (reaction/response). Have you ever met a hypochondriac? Every real or imagined thing seems to generate fear of serious illness. How about the smoker who ignores their persistent cough? Do you know anyone who imagines that no one likes them and therefore suffers from poor self-esteem? Do you know anyone who doesn't believe they can accomplish anything good and who never seems to enjoy success at anything? Have you ever met someone who is negative about everything? These are all common day to day examples of illness which is wrapped up in errors of perception, analysis, and interpretation, or in patterns of reaction and response that are unhealthy. **Frequently, these patterns of behavior are grounded on something purely imaginary!** Have you ever felt yourself getting angry remembering something that happened weeks ago? Have you ever experienced worry imagining that something bad will unfold later in the day?

In trying to attain a state of improved health, we are faced with a difficult task. It's difficult to examine the filters and blocks that distort our perception. To some extent we all see the world through rose (or some other) colored glasses. It's difficult to examine the software/programming that determines how accurately or inaccurately we analyze and interpret what we perceive. Our attitude essentially stems from these perceptual filters and analytic programming. What sort of lens do you view the world through? Do we see the glass as half empty or half full?

Furthermore, it is very difficult to step back and consider how we react and respond, what alternative reactions we might choose, and to decide to make the healthiest response. **We might think our choices are to get mad or get even, but a much healthier option is to get over**. We can make ourselves ill reprocessing past hurts or dwelling on imaginary future negative scenarios. This kind of reprocessing can generate destructive emotions such as anger or fear that we examined in the last chapter.

Sometimes our analytic programming leads to errors of interpretation which lead to unhealthy reactions and responses. Think of your "rules governing relationships" that I discussed in chapter ten. Those rules represent your software programming. Sometimes those programs really need to be rewritten. What do you see and how do you interpret everything that's going on around you and inside your head? What filters and blocks distort your perception? What programming determines your analysis? And how do these affect your reaction? All too often we see threats that don't exist, past present and future. We infer hurt that was never intended, we react with anger or fear or jealousy or spite, and respond in ways that ultimately cause suffering. Such suffering is needless. Often this suffering occurs in response to errors of perception, analysis, and judgment. It occurs as a result of ingrained attitudes and response patterns.

In our minds, we forge a link between pain and suffering. Such pain may be physical or mental or spiritual. To this pain we attach significance and with that attachment comes our suffering. Cancer can be physically painful as in the case of bone metastases. But the suffering may come from fear of the future, fear of more physical pain, fear of death. Or the suffering may come from feelings of guilt, that something we did brought the cancer upon ourselves. Or the suffering may come from feeling abandoned by God or distanced from our loved ones or alone in our struggle. These are the components of suffering which are linked to our pain. These links or attachments must be examined and understood so that we can break the unhealthy links and forge other healthy attachments.

That's the good news—we can reduce our suffering by making healthy choices. **Our neural circuits have an inherent plasticity; they can be reprogrammed**. While this is analogous to changing the software, the net effect over time is to actually change the neural circuits in our brain, i.e. the hardware. We are capable of learning new patterns of behavior and response. Ultimately, these changes can lead us to a place of better health. As I have said before, we can be our own worst enemy or our own best ally. Whose side do you want to be on?

In the same ways we link suffering to pain, **we link illness to disease**. Diabetes is a disease. Attached to that disease may be anger that this has happened, anger that there are dietary restrictions that now ought to be respected, guilt when that diet is not followed, fear of what the future might bring in the form of heart attack, kidney failure, or amputation. These are the attachments which generate suffering. Anger, guilt, and fear are the type of destructive thoughts and emotional responses which complicate our reaction to diseases and frequently define our illness experience. These reaction and response patterns are part of our software not our hardware and thus they can be reprogrammed. We can develop attitudes of hope and resiliency in the face of disease instead of attitudes of victimization and suffering. Does adversity motivate or demoralize you? When life is not going your way can you learn to "roll with the punches"?

Needless suffering and undo illness result from unhealthy response patterns. Think for a moment of some life circumstance and try to separate in your mind what represents the event and what represents your reaction. What significance do you attach to that life circumstance? Is it carried forward to the present in a way that impedes you from moving forward? Has it been written into your life story in a way that leads to continued reprocessing and response? Think of a medical problem you have and how your response to that medical problem has been either healthy or unhealthy. Are you stuck in a grief reaction or self-conditioned to a destructive emotional response? **Disease to which no significance is attached has no impact on health**. We are all capable of making, "A hell out of heaven and a heaven out of hell…" In the assessment section I shall ask you to consider whether you have helped to create a heavenly or a hellish reality for yourself and how this potentially affects your health.

So where does this programming come from? In much the same way as I discussed in the section on rules guiding relationships, your programming comes from beliefs and values, socialization, past experience, imprinting from childhood examples, and role modeling. Media advertising, television, and things you were taught in school also have all influenced your way of processing data from the world around you in order to create your reality. If you have reacted to a certain set of circumstances in a particular way (determined by how your programming processes information) chances are good you will have the same response pattern when represented with the same information. **In this way that reality is constantly reinforced**. If someone cut you off while driving to work caused you to react with anger, and you continue to replay this circumstance in your mind, it's very likely you will remain angry. In this example, maybe it was totally appropriate to be angry when this occurred, but the choice to revisit this repeatedly is a choice you make. **The healthy choice is to acknowledge it and move on**. Put it in the past. If you must relive it, challenge your response. You could have laughed when it happened instead of getting bent out of shape. That would have been a healthier choice.

If your software is programmed to worry when your child is out with friends and this leaves you feeling anxious or insecure (your response), chances are that this will continue unless you do some reprogramming. Reprogramming does not mean that you ignore possible problems which could happen—your child could be in an auto accident, get mugged, be around drugs. These are realities which you should be aware of. Reprogramming means that you change your response pattern in how you react to these realities. Instead of choosing to worry you choose not to worry, a healthy choice. These examples represent common real life circumstances. I'm sure you could substitute other events that have more relevance in your own life, but the point remains. **Our response/ reaction patterns are frequently programmed in ways that are unhealthy**.

It is difficult to step back, examine your reactivity, and begin to unravel why you behave the way you do. This is often the focus of psychotherapy, but you are absolutely capable of beginning to do this on your own. Here is a simple four step process to get you started:

First: Recognize and get in touch with your thoughts and feelings pertaining to a person, thing, or event, e.g. I feel confused, lonely, depressed, angry, sad, stressed, etc.

Second: Ask yourself why you have that thought or emotion. Keep asking why until you get to the root cause.

Third: Ask yourself what alternative healthier reactions/responses you could choose.

Fourth: Recognize the choice you are making presently and ask yourself what reasons deter you from making a better choice.

Let's consider an example: Your anniversary is coming up and you are nervous and upset. First recognize these feelings (I am aware that I am nervous/upset.) Next determine why you have these feelings—You are afraid your spouse will forget?—Why?—You are feeling insecure about the relationship in general—Why? You don't talk much anymore, your sex life has bombed, you argue all the time, etc. Okay, we could probably trace this example back further, but let's say the root cause is fear that the relationship has tanked. Next consider alternative reactions—discussion together, counseling, considering your own role in bringing the relationship to this place, things you can do to make the relationship better. Any of these are potentially healthier options for you to choose. Finally, recognize that you are making the choice. **The biggest barrier, the most important deterrent to making healthier choices is you.**

It's a lot easier to write this and suggest for you to give it a try than it is to actually go out and do it. It's especially hard at first because our programming is usually pretty well established and it requires effort to rethink and retrain ourselves. But, as I said previously, the human brain is remarkable and has plasticity. Therefore new neural circuits—think of these as a hardware upgrade, will develop in response to new software instructions. Then it gets a whole lot easier.

For some individuals, sickness has become incorporated into their self-image and psyche. Their illness, or pain, or anger eventually defines who they are and gives them an excuse to act the way they do. **Even though life and people can be very harsh, cruel and unfair, we still have options as to how we choose to deal with the harsh realities of life**. You can respond as a victim. You can blame all your problems on externals. Or, you can step back, examine what internal factors contribute to your problems and make healthy choices about how you respond. I encourage you to choose wisely. Try to program yourself to have an attitude of gratitude. That's a choice you can make. What's stopping you?

Chapter Fourteen:

Stress Management-Getting through an obstacle course

"Doctor, I feel very stressed!"

I cannot count the number of times I've been told that. Worse, I cannot count the number of times I have concluded someone is suffering from stress related illness, but the person hasn't made the connection. Headaches, fatigue, trouble sleeping, irritability, chest pain, abdominal pain…the list goes on…all potentially symptoms of stress.

Stressed out, mega stressed, stressed to the max; **stress is pervasive in our society**.

Nowhere are the principles of balance as a measure of health more relevant than when it comes to discussing stress and how we manage it, or not!

But what is stress? Although people talk about it all the time, frequently they do not have much understanding about what stress is and what it represents. How do you understand stress? How is stress affecting your health? Quite simply, **stress represents a physiologic reaction. It is a reaction to some stressor in our lives.** That stressor can be external to us, as in being chased by a mad dog. Or, it can be internal, as in worrying if you'll have enough money to pay this month's rent. In truth, our reaction to stress is an adaptive response to help enable us to temporarily perform at a higher than normal level. So, if you are a baseball player batting in the 9th inning with the bases loaded and your team behind (a stressful situation), your body releases some adrenaline which revs up your system and hopefully helps you to hit a home run. Or, if you are about to be mugged, the release of adrenaline helps you to run fast and far to get away. Or, if you've got an important deadline to meet for a project at work your body's response helps you to be sharp, to stay up late, remain focused and meet your deadline.

Many people have heard of the "fight or flight" response which simply describes this physiologic, adaptive reaction to dealing with a stressful situation. Short term, this is good, and, as I've said, it helps us perform at our best. Faced with continued stressors, the body continues to release these "stress hormones", usually with adverse results—high blood pressure, chronic fatigue, trouble sleeping, irritability, relationship problems, feeling overwhelmed, and/or a whole host of other unhealthy consequences.

Unfortunately, we live in a fast paced, high pressure world and dealing with chronic stressors is more the norm than the exception. So how do we deal with this reality and stay healthy? How do we cope with all the stressors in our lives? How do you cope?

In no sections of this guidebook are the principals of balance more relevant than in the discussion of stress management. So many of the ideas that I have already asked you to consider are fundamental to successfully managing the many stressors that undoubtedly affect your health and well-being. These stressors are like obstacles both within and without that you can learn to negotiate around. In this final chapter, prior to beginning the self-assessment exercises, you will understand how your ability to successfully manage the stressors in your life, **without feeling stressed**, relates to physical, mental, emotional, spiritual, and environmental factors.

To help you, I am asking that you imagine a large container. Into this container flows a liquid. The container can be big or small. The liquid can flow in fast or slow. No matter how big/small, fast/slow, **sooner or later the container will overflow**. Think of the container as a person's innate ability to handle stress and think of the liquid flowing in as the various stressors that person has to contend with. No matter how big the person's stress container is and no matter how many or few the stressors are, sooner or later the container overflows. When the container overflows the person suffers unhealthy consequences, specifically, stress related signs or symptoms of illness. Chest pain, abdominal pain, headaches, anxiety, depression, anger, poor job performance, poor life performance, strained marriages, suicide, irritable bowel syndrome, feeling unwell, feeling overwhelmed, unhappy, unmotivated, etc., etc.—all are potentially related to a container that has, quite simply, over flown.

On the dashboard of your car are lights which indicate a possible mechanical problem. They may sometimes flash or blink with information like: "check engine" or "oil pressure low". These are referred to as "idiot lights". Failing to pay attention to these lights could have disastrous consequences for your car; you may even have a total breakdown by not heeding the warning. Don't ignore those flashing lights on your dashboard. Well, the human body is a lot more complicated than an automobile. Even more than the car you drive, your body has a lot of monitoring systems and a lot of ways to tell you something is wrong. Many of these systems tell us something is wrong before we have an actual breakdown. We need to recognize those warnings. Often they are some of the very things I've listed as occurring with poorly managed stress.

In my experience as a primary doctor, stress related health problems are far and away the most common problems affecting my patients. I suspect you are no different.

The following diagram illustrates the container model:

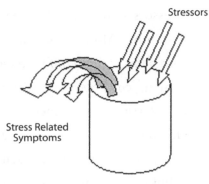

Allostasis defines your ability to maintain physiologic balance in response to various stressors. The greater the number, intensity, and duration of stressors the greater your allostatic load. A high allostatic load correlates with poor health i.e. increased morbidity and mortality. Bottom line—a high allostatic load is bad and reducing your allostatic load is good.

So what are the common stressors most people have to contend with? They include things like work pressures, family/household difficulties, financial pressures and time management. Some of these may be **external**, such as a leaky roof with no money in the budget to do repairs, or a co-worker who is abrasive, or a noisy and chaotic home environment, or a nagging spouse. Frequently these stressors are **internal**, such as fear that your teenager will be in a car accident, or dissatisfaction with your job or pay, or the feeling that other people don't like you.

My intent in discussing this with you is to help you see what the stressors in your life are. Some of the stressors are beyond your ability to control e.g. if there isn't enough money in the budget to fix the leaky roof you will need to contend with both the financial stress and the water in the house. If your parent is dying of cancer and depending on your help, let's face it, that's a situation you cannot control. But some of the circumstances that generate stress in your life you can control. If you are overextended with commitments and are feeling there isn't enough time, perhaps you can simplify. Reexamine some of those financial stressors and see if you can be happy with less. Work on your relationships. If you are spiritually in a morass, do something to reconnect. If driving to work frequently stresses you out because of traffic, maybe you can take a different route which might be longer but less stressful.

It is helpful to categorize your stressors, both internal and external. For most people, stressors are present at work and/or at home. Money and time management usually are categories to consider. Relationship problems and/or conflict typically affect most people. These can be with spouse, children, parents, coworkers or just about anyone you deal with regularly or is significant in your life. Worries about something are commonly a source for stress. Some people without much money worry about whether they can pay their bills. Many people with plenty of money still worry about having enough. You may be worried that your kid is using drugs, but maybe that worry is misplaced.

It is helpful to specifically list the stressors in your life and to rate them on a scale of one to five (one less stressful, five very stressful). Some life circumstances are known to be highly stressful such as death of a spouse, divorce, or moving. It also helps to indicate whether the item is or is not within your ability to change. To help you organize your stressors, I've got you started with the table below:

STRESSORS	INTERNAL/EXTERNAL OR BOTH	RATE 1-5	ABILITY TO CHANGE: HIGH/LOW
Relationships			
Time Management			
Money			
Worries			
Other			
Other			

Thus far, we've spent some time examining the stress response, common stress related health problems, and typical life stressors. I've asked you to individualize things according to your specific life circumstances. The real challenge to getting through the obstacle course of stress lies in how we manage those stressors. **Stress management enables you to prevent your container from overflowing**. And stress management is a highly individualized affair. It affords a good opportunity to take an integral approach.

So far I've told you about all the things filling up your container. The good news is that there is a spigot at the bottom of the container which you can open up to let it drain. And **you control the spigot**. In other words, you can open it as wide or as small as you choose and you determine how well and how fast your container drains. This spigot is the key to reducing your allostatic load.

While many of the factors you have already listed are beyond your ability to control, and therefore the liquid may be pouring in, even gushing in to your stress container, you have the ability to open that spigot as wide as you choose. And, if indeed the water is flowing in fast, **you will need to drain it just as fast or it will overflow**. The balance you seek is a point below the overflow mark. This is the range where your health is not suffering. I've diagrammed it for you below:

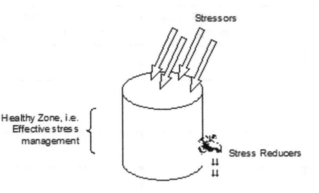

A common experience for people suffering from stress is that they **feel overwhelmed and out of control**. Just understanding that you can still have all the same stressors (what's pouring into your bucket) and not feel stressed (by managing the drain emptying your bucket) can be very liberating. So how do you do this? There are many strategies, any of which separately or in combination, you can follow to effectively empty your stress container. They are all the sorts of things we have been discussing. In the physical realm: good diet and exercise habits, getting enough sleep, relinquishing unhealthy habits like smoking and drinking too much, going for a massage; all of these can help to relieve stress. In the mental and emotional realm: spending time with enjoyable past times, or hobbies, allowing yourself protected downtime, nurturing relationships, forgiving, playing, watching a funny movie; any of these can help to open up the spigot that drains the stored up stress. Confiding in a friend, relative, or someone you trust can help to get things "off your chest". While it's true that those stressors will still be present, you will likely feel better. Confront the conflict in your life instead of letting it fester. It's like toxic waste you are holding inside and it's poisoning you. Examine your reactivity and perform an "attitude adjustment". Go for counseling. Recast yourself out of the victim role.

In the spiritual realm, anything you do that connects you to Source will reduce the stress you feel. This might include, prayer, meditation, a walk in the woods, acknowledging the blessings in your life, or focusing with awe, reverence, and appreciation for the wonder of creation. Look around at your environment. Clean up the clutter. Turn off the TV. Understand how you have been subjected to ceaseless advertising giving you the message that you need to buy something in order to be happy. Volunteer in your community. All of these actions are within your control. These actions represent an integral approach to dealing with the stressors in your life. **Choosing to manage your stress and recognizing that you can indeed regain the balance you seek are within your ability.** You control the spigot!

The more stressors people are contending with in life, the less time and effort they tend to apply towards stress management. Has this occurred in your life? Can you appreciate that the more stressors you are contending with, the greater is your need to spend time actively opening the drain by some combination of body, mind, spirit, environmental rebalancing?

Sadly, there are other paths people take in an effort to contend with stress. These include: yelling, fighting, violence, thrill seeking, shopping therapy (often leading to more financial stress.) Substance abuse—both legally with tobacco, alcohol, and prescription medication and illegally with street drugs and sexual misconduct may represent other strategies for dealing with stress. I've discussed some of these previously in the chapter on addictions. And while it might temporarily feel good to drain your container a little by kicking the dog or your partner or your kids, or to get high, or light up, or have a one night stand, or buy something expensive that you don't really need, these choices are not a healthy way to manage stress and frequently wind up causing more stress in a person's life. If the examples above are part of your coping strategies, I hope you can see other healthy alternatives to choose as you try to manage the stress in your life. Part Four in this guidebook will offer you some suggestions.

A final word for women who suffer from PMS, the container model provides a useful conceptual framework to consider in trying to understand some of the common symptoms accompanying PMS. Symptoms such as mood swings, irritability, negativity, impatience, sleep disturbance are all commonly experienced as manifestations of stress which is not being effectively managed. These same symptoms may occur in association with PMS. I have sometimes asked patients who suffer from PMS to think of themselves as having two different stress containers. The large container is operating for most of the month, but they may have a much smaller container for the time of the month close to their menses. Accordingly, the need for more aggressive stress management, by focusing on how to open the spigot wide during this time of the month, can sometimes help ameliorate these symptoms. Understanding your body's natural rhythms is especially important if you experience PMS. Remember, your body is trying to tell you something. Pay close attention to your cycle. Try not to schedule your child's birthday party when you can expect to be close to your menses. Schedule extra protected time or more exercise or some treat for yourself such as a massage for times when you anticipate you might experience premenstrual symptoms. Instead of feeling at the mercy of your body's hormonal fluctuations, you can learn to regain some balance and harmony by your awareness and application of these stress management techniques.

If your body is trying to tell you something about stress, much like the idiot lights on the dashboard of your car, don't wait for a breakdown. Take stock of your stressors and examine your stress management strategies. Think of the container model and of balance. Sit down. Slow down. Go for a walk. Go for a bicycle ride. Take a ride in your car with no destination in mind. Pray. Laugh. Repair broken relationships. Spend time with your loved ones. Watch the sunset. Reprioritize. Make healthy choices. Forgive. Regain a sense of control. Appreciate life…it's precious.

Part Three:
MAP YOUR HEALTH
MISSION DESIGNER

Taking Stock to Get Your Bearings

Photo courtesy Paul Schnaittacher

VIDEO LINK #4 IN APPENDIX

DOWNLOAD AND PRINT MAP KEY ASSESSMENTS IN APPENDIX

Chapter Fifteen:

General Questions and Exercises-Map Key #1

With a new, integral appreciation of health you can now begin to take inventory of the state of your own health. Take time answering the questions that follow and in performing the exercises. Your goal is to take a snapshot of where you are currently located on the map of your health. Using this information will help you to chart a course to arrive at a place of better health. There are no right or wrong answers to these questions. Be honest.

ON A SCALE OF 1—10 HOW DO YOU RATE YOUR HEALTH?

*Sickly **1*** _____ ***10*** *Optimum Health*

WHAT NEEDS TO CHANGE TO MOVE FROM YOUR CURRENT TO A HIGHER SCORE?

_____

_____

_____

_____

_____

WHEN DID YOU LAST FEEL WELL? _____

FILL IN YOUR HEALTH SCORE (1—10) ON THE TIMELINE BELOW

Now fill in some important life events on the same time line. These events might include things such as childhood illness, trauma, death of a loved one, breakup of a significant relationship, marriage, becoming a parent, etc.

I've given you an example below:

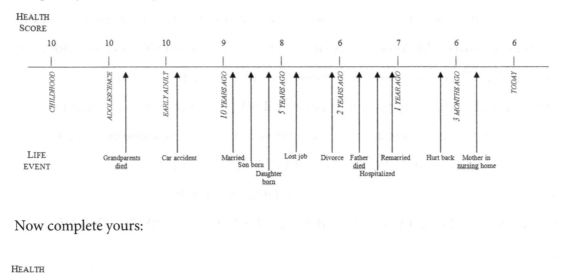

Now complete yours:

Can you see any correlation between your overall health score as it relates to significant events in your life?

If the answer is yes, explain:_____

List below your current diagnoses for any health problems:

_____

_____

_____

_____

List below any prescription medications which you take regularly:

_____

_____

_____

What do you expect these medications to achieve?_____

_____

Are your expectations for what your medications are intended to achieve being met? If not, why not? _____

_____

_____

List below non-prescription medications, vitamins, pills, or supplements that you take regularly:

_____

_____

_____

What additional health problems do you have which are not included in your list of diagnoses?

_____

_____

_____

What do you expect these pills to achieve?_____

_____

Are your expectations for what your pills are intended to achieve being met? If not, why not?_____

_____

Exercise—Map Key #1 (be as complete as possible in filling out the table)

Review your list of diagnoses and other health problems which you have listed above and complete the table below. The column for "Impact" asks how this affects your daily life (e.g. if you have chronic back pain the impact may be, "Prevents me from playing tennis, being as active as I would like to be"). The column for "Significance" asks why the impact is important to you (e.g. having high blood pressure may have little impact on your day to day life but important significance such as, "Concerned about causing heart attack/stroke" or " Don't like to take medication").

Health Problem/ Diagnosis:	Onset:	Impact:	Significance:

(as you work through later assessments you may need to attach additional pages to this table)

Great! You have taken an important step forward towards your goal of achieving better health. Have you learned anything, about your health?

You will use the above and other Map Keys to construct an individualized map of your health in the final exercise in this guidebook. The more details you discover and record, the better your map will describe the territory of your health. Consequently, the better equipped you will be to chart a course to improved health and well-being.

1ST MAP KEY VIDEO IN APPENDIX

Chapter Sixteen:

Body Questions and Exercises-Map Key #2

Let's take a look at your means of transportation. Is it well cared for and maintained? Are there worsening signs of wear and tear or impending breakdown? Are you stranded on the side of the road?

ON A SCALE OF 1—10, RATE YOUR PHYSICAL HEALTH.

Poor 1 _____ *10 Excellent*

DO YOU FEEL THAT YOUR CURRENT WEIGHT IS HEALTHY FOR YOU? _____

    IF NOT, WHY NOT? _____

    HOW IS YOUR WEIGHT DIFFERENT THAN FIVE YEARS AGO?

_____

DO YOU FEEL THAT YOUR CURRENT DIET IS WELL BALANCED AND HEALTHY?

_____

DO YOU EAT THREE MEALS A DAY? _____

DO YOU SNACK BETWEEN MEALS? _____

ARE YOUR MEAL AND SNACK CHOICES HEALTHY? _____

    IF NOT, WHY NOT? _____

LIST YOUR LAST THREE MEALS AND INDICATE WHETHER YOU FEEL THEY ARE OR ARE NOT HEALTHY:

_____

_____

_____

_____

WHAT BEVERAGES DO YOU TYPICALLY DRINK THROUGHOUT THE DAY?

_____

How many servings of soda do you typically consume in a week?_____

      Do you think your beverage choices are healthy?_____

How active are you in your typical work and leisure activities?

___sedentary___some activity ___active ___very active

How often do you engage in exercise?_____

Does pain limit your physical activity?_____

Do you have problems when you exert yourself physically?

      If yes, how so?_____

Compared to five years ago are more active___less active___ About the same___?

      If your activity has changed, why?_____

      Do you think your exercise/activity patterns are healthy?_____

How much sleep do you require per night to feel well rested?_____

      How much sleep do you typically get per night?_____

If you require more sleep per night than you typically get, what is the reason for this?___

_____

Do you frequently feel fatigued?_____

      If yes, is this mostly a feeling of lack of energy___, sleepiness___, or both___?

What are things you do which boost your energy level?

_____

_____

What are things you do which lower your energy level?

_____

_____

Do you smoke?_____ Do you use recreational drugs?_____

How many servings of alcoholic beverages do you consume in a typical week?_____

Do you respect your physical body's needs?_____

Do you sometimes feel that you abuse your physical body?_____

     If yes, why?_____

If you could step outside yourself and interview your physical body, what would your body want to tell you?

_____

_____

_____

_____

Map Key #2

What habits or activities do you do which you feel help you to be healthier?

_____

_____

What prevents you from doing these more often?

_____

_____

What habits or activities do you do which you feel diminish your health?

_____

_____

Why do you do these?_____

What prevents you from stopping or doing these less?_____

_____

Overall do you feel physically well balanced? ___yes ___no

What aspects of your physical body are out of balance?_____

_____

Update Map Key #1 with any additional health problems you have uncovered

2ND MAP KEY VIDEO IN APPENDIX

Chapter Seventeen:

Mind Questions and Exercises-Map Key #3

Now it's time to look at pilot and navigator. Are you moving forward, backward, or around in circles? Are you lost? Where are you headed?

Do you experience trouble thinking clearly? _____

  If yes, describe how/why:_____

_____

Do you experience trouble with your memory?_____

Do you experience trouble focusing or staying on task?_____

  If yes, describe how/why:_____

_____

Do you experience difficulty making decisions?

  If yes, describe how/why:_____

Is it more difficult for you to understand things than for most other people?_____

How intelligent do you rate yourself?

___below average ___average ___above average ___far above average.

What things do you do to stimulate your mind?_____

_____

Are you satisfied with your level of mental stimulation?_____

If not, why not?_____

On a scale of 1—10 rate your typical level of happiness:

Unhappy 1 _____ *10 Very Happy*

On the following timeline, indicate your happiness score:

HAPPINESS
SCORE

CHILDHOOD	ADOLESCENCE	EARLY ADULT	10 YEARS AGO	5 YEARS AGO	2 YEARS AGO	1 YEAR AGO	3 MONTHS AGO	TODAY

WHAT ARE THINGS IN YOUR LIFE WHICH INCREASE YOUR HAPPINESS? INCLUDE WHY
THESE THINGS MAKE YOU HAPPIER:

_____

_____

_____

_____

_____

_____

WHAT ARE THINGS IN YOUR LIFE WHICH DECREASE YOUR HAPPINESS? INCLUDE WHY
THESE THINGS MAKE YOU LESS HAPPY:

_____

_____

_____

_____

_____

_____

WHAT PERCENTAGE OF YOUR TYPICAL DAY DO YOU FEEL UPBEAT? _____

LIST PEOPLE, THINGS, CIRCUMSTANCES WHICH GENERATE ANGER THAT IS HIGH INTENSITY,

HIGH FREQUENCY, OR PERSISTENT IN DURATION: _____

_____

_____

_____

_____

WHAT "INTERNAL RULES" HAVE BEEN VIOLATED IN THE EXAMPLES ABOVE?

_____

_____

_____

_____

_____

_____

DOES FEELING ANGRY MAKE YOU FEEL GOOD? _____ARE YOU ADDICTED TO FEELING

ANGRY?_____

DO YOU THINK BEING ANGRY IS HEALTHY?_____

WHAT THINGS DO YOU DO TO REDUCE YOUR ANGER?_____

_____

_____

HAVE ANY OF THESE ANGER REDUCING STRATEGIES BECOME ADDICTIONS?_____

3A. **Review your anger list and consider healthy choices you can make to reduce or eliminate anger. This can include deciding not to get angry, ways of minimizing anger, or both. Complete the following table:**

Anger Source:	Intensity: (high/low)	Frequency: (often/rare)	Duration: (long/short)	Healthy Alternatives

LIST PEOPLE, THINGS, CIRCUMSTANCES WHICH CAUSE FEAR, WORRY, OR ANXIETY THAT IS HIGH INTENSITY, HIGH FREQUENCY, OR PERSISTENT IN DURATION:_____

_____

_____

_____

_____

WHY ARE YOU AFRAID, WORRIED, ANXIOUS ABOUT THESE THINGS?_____

_____

DO YOUR FEARS, WORRIES, OR ANXIETIES MAKE YOU FEEL HEALTHY? _____

HAVE FEAR/WORRY/ANXIETY BECOME AN UNHEALTHY RESPONSE PATTERN

FOR YOU? _____

WHAT THINGS DO YOU DO TO REDUCE FEAR/WORRY/ANXIETY? _____

_____

Have any of these become addictive?_____

DO YOU UNDERSTAND THAT FEELING AFRAID, WORRIED, OR ANXIOUS IS A CHOICE YOU

MAKE?_____

3B. What healthy choices or strategies are you willing to try to help reduce fear/worry/anxiety?_____

_____

_____

What other negative emotions such as hatred, guilt, jealousy, shame, etc. are causing you imbalance?_____

_____

What healthy choices or strategies are you willing to try to help reduce these negative feelings?_____

_____

WHEN YOU CONSIDER THE WORKINGS OF YOUR MIND—THOUGHTS AND EMOTIONS, HOW

BALANCED DO YOU FEEL? _____

Why? _____

3C. What positive emotions would you like to experience more often:

_____

_____

_____

What can you do to experience these positive emotions more often?

_____

_____

_____

What can you do to improve your mental health?

_____

_____

Who can assist you in these efforts?_____

_____

Sections 3A, 3B, and 3C above are your Map Key #3

Update Map Key #1 with any additional mental health problems you have uncovered

3RD MAP KEY VIDEO IN APPENDIX

Chapter Eighteen:

Spirit Questions and Exercises-Map Key #4

Spirit is moving you right now to examine the Integral connections that affect your health.

Let's examine your spirit and find out what's moving you.

ON A SCALE OF 1—10 HOW SPIRITUAL ARE YOU?

*Not Spiritual 1*_____ **10** *Very Spiritual*

What are your beliefs about creation?_____

_____

Do you consider yourself a "person of faith"?_____

Do you believe in God, a supreme being, or Source consciousness?_____

Explain how this belief impacts your health:_____

_____

How do you relate to or interact with God/supreme being/Source consciousness?

_____

Do you sometimes feel you deserve to be punished by God or that you are somehow being punished by God? _____

    If yes, explain why or how: _____

_____

Do you belong to an organized religion?_____

    If not, why not?_____

    If yes, do you participate regularly in your religion?_____

        If not, why not? _____

Do you experience times of expanded consciousness?_____

    If yes, describe these: _____

_____

Have you ever had a mystical experience? _____

    If yes, what have you learned from the experience? _____

_____

Do you have a set of "core values" or "guiding principles"?

    If yes, list them: _____

_____

_____

    How well aligned are you with these core values or guiding principles?

    ___not very___relatively aligned___highly aligned

    What could you do to improve your alignment?_____

_____

What do you believe is your purpose in life? _____

_____

How well aligned are you with this purpose?

___not very___relatively aligned___highly aligned

If you are not well aligned, why? _____

_____

Do you believe you have a "higher purpose" which is somehow related to God? _____

    If yes, explain this relationship:_____

    _____

    If yes, how well aligned are you with this purpose?

    ___not very___relatively   aligned___highly aligned

    How does this make you feel? _____

    _____

Do you pray? _____

    If yes, are you satisfied with your prayer life? _____

    If not, why not?_____

Do you meditate? _____

    If yes, are you satisfied with your meditation practice? _____

    If not, why not? _____

How do you nourish your soul? _____

_____

How do you connect with the Divine? _____

_____

On a scale of 1—10 how do you rate the health of your soul? _____

    Poor 1 _____*10 Excellent*

Do you feel you can do more to nourish your soul or spend more time connecting with

the Divine? _____

    If yes, why don't you?_____

How do your spirit and your body interact? _____

_____

How does your spirit inform your thoughts and emotions? _____

_____

How well balanced do you fell spiritually? ___not very___pretty well___

highly balanced___

Map Key #4

List the areas of your spirituality which you feel are important to your health:

- _____

- _____

- _____

Why are these important to you?_____

_____

What would you like to do to improve your spiritual health?

- _____

- _____

Update Map Key #1 with any additional spiritual problems you have uncovered

4TH MAP KEY VIDEO IN APPENDIX

4TH MAP KEY VIDEO IN APPENDIX

Chapter Nineteen:

Environment Questions and Exercises–Map Key #5

The territory you are traveling in is pretty complicated. Your world has many unique features. Let's look around and examine them in some more detail.

LOOK, LISTEN, SMELL AND TOUCH WHERE YOU ARE RIGHT AT THIS MOMENT.

Is it visually pleasing?_____ Messy and chaotic?_____

Are the sounds around you soothing or do you need to block them out? _____

Are the smells good and comforting or unpleasant? _____

Do you frequently breathe artificial smells or chemicals? _____

Is the place you are in somewhere you want to reach out, touch, and explore?_____

Ask the same questions about places where you live—your bedroom, kitchen, family room, etc. What do you conclude about how healthy these places are?

_____

_____

How about your work environment?_____ How about your car?_____

Do they comfort your senses or offend them? _____

Natural lighting is healthier than artificial. How do you light the world around you?_____

_____

Do you think it's important to try and make your physical environment as healthy as you possibly can? _____

What do your senses tell you about the different physical environments where you commonly spend time?_____

5A. Are there things you can do to make these places healthier? List them now:

- _____

- _____

- _____

- _____

- _____

ON A SCALE OF 1—10 RATE YOUR VIEW OF THE WORLD AROUND YOU.

*Scary/Threatening **1**_____**10** Safe/Nurturing*

WHAT IS YOUR SOCIOECONOMIC STATUS?_____ YOUR RACE? _____YOUR ETHNIC BACKGROUND? _____

DO YOU BELONG TO ANY COMMUNITY GROUPS OR ORGANIZATIONS?_____

IF NOT, WHY NOT?_____

IS YOUR NEIGHBORHOOD SAFE? _____

DO YOU DO ANY VOLUNTEER WORK? _____ IF NOT, WOULD YOU BE WILLING TO START VOLUNTEERING? _____

HOW DO YOU SEE YOURSELF AS HELPING TO IMPROVE THE HEALTH OF YOUR COMMUNITY?

_____

DO YOU THINK YOUR HEALTH WILL BENEFIT FROM HELPING YOUR COMMUNITY? _____

5B. List some social and cultural factors which affect your health and how you think about health and why these are important to you (*if you are struggling to answer this, review the section on environment*):

- _____
- _____
- _____
- _____

List things you are willing to do to make your neighborhood, community, or the world a better place:

- _____
- _____
- _____
- _____

HOW DO YOU RATE THE QUALITY OF YOUR RELATIONSHIPS IN GENERAL?

____POOR____FAIR____GOOD

IF YOU WERE ILL, DO YOU HAVE FRIENDS OR FAMILY CLOSE BY WHO WOULD HELP YOU AND/OR CHECK ON YOU? _____

Some of the following questions may not apply to everyone

Describe the quality of your relationship with your spouse or significant other:

_____

Are there areas of ongoing conflict? _____

How do these conflicts relate to different expectations in your rulebooks of behavior? _____

_____

Have you dug in to your position? _____ Retreated? _____

Would you like this relationship to be better? _____

Do you think your health would benefit if this relationship was better? _____

What are you doing to make it better?_____

Describe the quality of your relationships with your boss and/or coworkers:

_____

What areas of conflict can you identify? _____

What are you doing to help resolve these conflicts? _____

_____

Describe the quality of your relationships with your parents, siblings, and children.

_____

List areas of conflict: _____

_____

Would you like any of these relationships to be better? _____

THINK OF PEOPLE YOU ARE FEELING ANGRY TOWARDS, DON'T LIKE, FEEL HURT BY, OR IN SOME WAY FEEL NEGATIVE ABOUT. WHY DO YOU FEEL THAT WAY TOWARDS THOSE INDIVIDUALS? _____

_____

ARE THERE ANY SIGNIFICANT RELATIONSHIPS (EITHER DETAILED ABOVE OR OTHER) WHICH ARE CAUSING YOU PAIN? _____

Review the section on relationships.

5C. List specific relationship issues which you feel affect your health and how they affect your health:

Issue	Affect:

Sections 5A, 5B, and 5C above are your Map Key #5

Update Map Key #1 with any additional environmental problems you have uncovered

5TH MAP KEY VIDEO IN APPENDIX

Chapter Twenty:

Final Questions and Exercises-Master Key

Almost there! This final assessment section is, in some sense, the most difficult because it challenges you to take a hard look at some deeply personal and internal issues. Motivation, addictions, forgiveness, grief, attitudes/perspectives and stress management are important areas to more fully understand when integrally assessing your health. Spend some extra time on this section. Your efforts will be rewarded.

LIST SOME OF THE THINGS YOU WOULD LIKE TO ACCOMPLISH OR ACHIEVE:

_____

_____

_____

_____

_____

_____

_____

_____

_____

From this list, select items which you feel that by achieving this goal your health will benefit. Then list specific internal and external motivators which will help you achieve this goal. (review the section on motivation for discussion of internal/external motivators if you are having trouble completing the table)

6A.

Goal	Internal Motivators	External Motivators

(as you work through this last assessment, attach additional pages to this table if needed)

Are you disciplined in your efforts to sustain motivation? _____

If not, what needs to change to help you have this discipline? _____

_____

When your motivation weakens or fails, what strategies will you use in order to persevere or to succeed? _____

_____

Who will you ask to help you improve your motivation and achieve your goals? _____

_____

_____

LIST THINGS WHICH YOU DO THAT YOU CONSIDER TO BE UNHEALTHY HABITS:

_____

_____

WHAT ACTIVITIES OR SUBSTANCES ARE YOU USING TO COUNTERACT DYSPHORIA OR TO INDUCE EUPHORIA OR IN SOME WAY TO "ESCAPE" THE PRESENT? _____

_____

_____

WHAT UNDERLYING STATE OR STATES ARE YOU TRYING TO CHANGE? _____

_____

_____

PLACE A CHECK MARK NEXT TO ANY THAT REPRESENT ADDICTIONS.

PLACE A STAR NEXT TO ANY THAT REPRESENT UNHEALTHY CHOICES.

CIRCLE ANY CHECKED OR STARRED ITEMS THAT YOU ARE MOTIVATED TO CHANGE.

FOR ANY CHECKED OR STARRED ITEMS YOUHAVE NOT CIRCLED, WHY ARE YOU NOT MOTIVATED TO CHANGE YOUR BEHAVIOR?_____

_____

LIST HEALTHIER WAYS FOR YOU TO DEAL WITH SITUATIONS YOU ARE TRYING TO ESCAPE OR STATES YOU ARE TRYING TO CHANGE: _____

_____

_____

Update section 6A with any additional goals pertaining to unhealthy habits or addictions.

LIST PEOPLE AND/OR SITUATIONS WHICH HAVE CAUSED YOU HURT THAT YOU HAVE NOT YET

FORGIVEN:_____

_____

_____

CONSIDER TIMES IN YOUR LIFE WHEN YOU HAVE CHOSEN NOT TO FORGIVE. WHAT HAS BEEN

THE RESULT/IMPACT OF THIS CHOICE?_____

_____

HOW IS FAILING TO FORGIVE CONTRIBUTING TO YOUR SUFFERING?_____

_____

DO YOU THINK THE CHOICE TO FORGIVE WILL BENEFIT YOUR HEALTH? _____

WHAT ARE YOUR CURRENT STRATEGIES FOR FORGIVENESS?_____

_____

DO THEY WORK? _____

LIST ANY AREAS OF SELF FORGIVENESS WHICH YOU WOULD LIKE TO WORK ON:_____

_____

HOW COULD AN ATTITUDE OF FORGIVENESS REDUCE WORLD CONFLICT AND IMPROVE

THE WORLD IN WHICH WE LIVE? _____

_____

_____

HOW CAN YOU CONTRIBUTE TO THIS? _____

_____

6B. List anything you feel you need to forgive. This applies to self, God, other people, life or world circumstances:

- _____
- _____
- _____
- _____

For any item listed above for which you are not willing at this time to choose forgiveness, why do you choose not to forgive?

- _____
- _____

     Does this bring you peace? _____

Update Section 6A with any additional goals related to forgiveness.

LIST BELOW SIGNIFICANT LOSSES YOU HAVE EXPERIENCED WHICH YOU THINK MAY BE AFFECTING YOUR HEALTH TODAY:_____

_____

_____

WHAT LOSSES ARE YOU STILL GRIEVING? _____

_____

HOW DO YOU RESPOND TO LOSS?_____

WHAT SOCIAL AND/OR CULTURAL ISSUES AFFECT YOUR ABILITY TO GRIEVE?_____

_____

DETAIL BELOW ANY SIGNIFICANT PHYSICAL, EMOTIONAL, OR SPIRITUAL TRAUMA YOU HAVE EXPERIENCED:_____

_____

_____

PLACE A CHECK NEXT TO ANY ITEM ABOVE WHICH STILL REQUIRES YOUR FORGIVENESS.
PLACE A STAR NEXT TO ANY ITEM ABOVE WHICH REPRESENTS AN AREA OF UNRESOLVED GRIEF.

6C. From what you have learned about grief, list ways you can improve your health in dealing with loss:

• _____

• _____

Update Section 6A with any additional goals related to grief.

DO YOU BELIEVE THAT YOU CAN ENJOY GOOD HEALTH? _____

    IF NOT, WHY NOT?_____

    _____

DO YOU SEE YOURSELF AS A HEALTHY PERSON? _____

    IF NOT, WHY NOT? _____

DO YOU BELIEVE IN THE "POWER OF POSITIVE THINKING"? _____

WHAT BELIEFS ABOUT YOUR HEALTH DO YOU HAVE WHICH YOU THINK ARE UNHEALTHY?

_____

_____

DO YOU FREQUENTLY SEE YOURSELF AS A VICTIM? _____

DO YOU BLAME OTHER PEOPLE OR EXTERNAL CIRCUMSTANCES FOR YOUR PROBLEMS?

_____

WHAT UNHEALTHY INTERNAL PROGRAMMING OR RESPONSE PATTERNS ARE YOU AWARE OF?_____

_____

HOW CAN YOU CHANGE THESE?_____

_____

ARE YOU MOTIVATED TO MAKE THESE CHANGES? _____ IF NOT, WHY NOT?_____

_____

WHO CAN YOU ASK TO HELP YOU MAKE THESE CHANGES? _____

_____

WOULD YOU LIKE TO HAVE A MORE POSITIVE ATTITUDE ABOUT YOUR HEALTH? _____

WHAT CAN YOU DO TO PROMOTE THIS?_____

_____

6D. What aspects of beliefs, attitudes, or perspectives about your health are areas which you would like to improve?

- _____

- _____

- _____

Update Section 6A with any additional goals related to attitude and perspective.

HOW DO YOU THINK STRESS IS AFFECTING YOUR HEALTH? _____

_____

_____

DO YOU SOMETIMES FEEL OVERWHELMED BY STRESS? _____

DO THE STRESSORS IN YOUR LIFE LEAVE YOU FEELING DISEMPOWERED OR "OUT OF CONTROL"? _____

IS IT IMPORTANT TO YOU TO FEEL "IN CONTROL" OF YOUR LIFE? _____

WHAT HAPPENS WHEN YOU NO LONGER FEEL IN CONTROL? _____

_____

LIST EXTERNAL FACTORS WHICH YOU FEEL ARE STRESSORS IN YOUR LIFE: _____

_____

_____

LIST INTERNAL FACTORS WHICH YOU FEEL ARE STRESSORS IN YOUR LIFE: _____

_____

_____

IN THE ABOVE LISTS, CIRCLE EXTERNAL AND INTERNAL STRESSORS WHICH YOU FEEL YOU

CAN CHANGE.

FOR THE ITEMS CIRCLED, EXPLAIN THINGS THAT YOU CAN DO TO CHANGE THINGS FOR

THE BETTER: _____

_____

_____

WHAT CURRENT STRATEGIES ARE YOU USING TO MANAGE STRESS? _____

_____

_____

HOW WELL ARE THEY WORKING?_____

FROM THE PRECEDING LIST, PLACE AN "X" THROUGH ANY STRATEGIES WHICH YOU JUDGE

TO BE   UNHEALTHY CHOICES TO HELP YOU COPE.

6E. List Body, Mind, Spirit, and Environmental things you can do to better manage your stress. This can include eliminating certain stressors in addition to selecting healthy choices to help you cope with the stressors in your life.

- _____
- _____
- _____
- _____
- _____

What prevents you from doing the things on the list above more or more often?

- _____
- _____

Who can you obtain help from in your efforts to better manage stress?

- _____
- _____

Update Section 6A with any additional goals related to stress management

Sections 6 A thru E above are your Map Key #6

Update Map Key #1 with any additional problems you have uncovered during your answers to the questions about motivation, addictions, forgiveness, grief, attitudes/perspectives, and stress management.

6TH MAP KEY VIDEO IN APPENDIX

Part Four:
Healing Strategies–Food, Rest, and Shelter

Photo courtesy Paul Schnaittacher

This guidebook about health would be incomplete without paying some attention to healing. I've asked you to develop an integral perspective about what constitutes health. I've asked you to think about health in terms of balance and harmony. In our language, health shares origin with the words for whole and holy. **Healing is the way health is restored or improved**. Healing is the process of improving balance and harmony. To heal is to make whole or holy. Notice this is a verb. Verbs describe actions. What lies behind the action of healing? **All healing involves the movement or transfer of energy.**

A lengthy discussion about human energies is beyond the scope of this guidebook, but a few quick highlights will give you the basic idea. Our bodies rely on many different energy interactions. Mechanical and kinetic energy govern the movement of our bones, muscles, and joints. Biochemical energy underlies cellular metabolism. Our nervous system and heart rely on impulses conducted through electrical energy. We radiate heat. We absorb and process light. We recognize and process sound. These are the types of physical energies we are all accustomed to. But there are other more subtle levels of energies which underlie psychic processes such as thoughts and dreams and emotions. It's curious how our language describes some of these exchanges of subtle energy that characterize a person—magnetic personality, radiant with joy, beaming. We sometimes characterize interactions between individuals using words such as: chemical attraction, electricity, or good/bad vibes. We are all energetic beings living in a vast field of energy. We constantly experience different energy states as we go through the day, interacting with one another and the greater field of energy. Anything which promotes a better energy state constitutes a healing process. Previously when I have discussed disease or illness in terms of imbalance, what I am actually describing as imbalance is a state of reduced energy. Sickness depletes energy. **Healing restores balance by improving our energetic state.**

Let's examine some common healing experiences and the movement or transfer of energy. Your back is out of alignment and you are adjusted by a chiropractor. The adjustment occurs through the transfer of mechanical energy. You receive a prescription medication to treat an infection. Through biochemical effects, this antibiotic inhibits the growth of a harmful germ. A pain medication mimics the body's normal production of pain blockers augmenting the body's natural biochemical process to reduce pain. These examples are in the realm of physical energy.

Further examples from the realm of subtle energies include: a psychotherapist uncovers and helps to release an emotional block allowing improved flow psychic energy; an acupuncturist uses needles to redirect *chi* (life energy); a Reiki practitioner rebalances *chakras* (energy vortices that parallel the spine and brain). Subtle energy can also be directed from a distance. Such a non-local effect can be seen in healing which follows a group praying for someone else's recovery. While many people find it difficult to accept or understand such non-local effects, there is a body of scientific research pioneered by such notable physicians as Larry Dossey supporting the role of prayer in healing.

Viewed from an integral perspective, health involves physical, mental, emotional, spiritual, social, and cultural variables. **The same is true for healing**. Taking a nice long bath is physically and emotionally comforting and helps to restore your energy balance. Repairing a broken relationship fixes a hole which has been depleting your energy. Reconnecting spiritually nourishes your soul providing you with a much needed energy boost. Volunteering your time to a worthwhile cause helps you to feel good about yourself. Depending on your religious and cultural beliefs and practices, things such as going to confession, observing fasting rituals, or participating in healing ceremonies may all be important ways to restore energy balance. **As you develop such an integral understanding of healing, you will understand it as dynamic and in constant flux.** Certain events and circumstances—a poor night's sleep, chronic pain, stress at home, an angry encounter, poor working conditions, social isolation, etc., etc. all have the effect of draining or unbalancing your overall energetic state. Opportunities to boost and rebalance your energy are all around you—straighten out the clutter, call someone to apologize, watch a funny movie, spend some time in prayer, take a nap, take a hike, sit down, slow down….recharge!

While you have many opportunities to improve your balance, it is also important to seek advice and assistance from trained healers. There are many different approaches to restoring balance. In the remainder of this chapter, I shall summarize some common healing modalities. My purpose here is to give you a menu of sorts which will help guide you to a practitioner or to a practice which helps improve your health. By no means is this a comprehensive list.

Acupuncture is a technique which uses thin needles inserted at specific points to help redirect the flow of *chi (qi),* or life energy. The points correspond to places on meridians which describe the flow of this energy within people. This energy based modality is widely used in Chinese medicine and is very holistic in concept. When *chi* is not in balance, there are detrimental health effects. Acupuncture is intended to help restore a healthy balance.

Allopathic medicine represents traditional Western medical care. As described elsewhere in this manual, the focus is on diagnosing disease based on the presence or absence of certain signs and symptoms, and test results. Treatment is typically through medication or surgery designed to improve anatomy and physiology by correcting pathologic states. Familiar subspecialties include neurologists, cardiologists, urologists, proctologist, etc.

Aroma therapy uses various scents, oils, and essences used individually or in combination. These may be applied topically or dispersed into your environment to facilitate stress reduction, stimulate the flow of internal energies, reduce pain, alter mood, or combat infection.

Ayurvedic practitioners employ many different techniques to alter *prana* or life energy. The various techniques include massage, yoga, meditation, herbs, supplements, and methods of detoxification. These practices have been utilized for thousands of years to treat and prevent all manner of disease and illness.

Biofeedback utilizes high tech equipment to monitor physiologic parameters such as heart rate using sensor electrodes. This information is utilized by the patient to promote relaxation and reduce pain.

Chiropractic involves the manipulation and adjustment of muscles, bones, and joints to improve physical functioning and alignment. Such manipulations may be targeted to reduce painful musculoskeletal imbalance or promote healthy realignment. Traditional chiropractic has focused primarily on the spine; however, many chiropractors now utilize additional healing strategies such as nutritional counseling and the use of supplements to benefit health.

Counseling is performed by many health practitioners alone or in combination. There are many different types of counseling performed by various therapists with different skills and treatment methods. All counseling involves some dialogue between client and counselor to help uncover underlying causes of disturbances and work on specific treatment recommendations. Psychologists and social workers frequently perform counseling. There are many different specific therapies (e.g. behavior, cognitive, regression, sex, to name just a few).

Craniosacral therapy is based upon the flow of cerebrospinal fluid, the fluid which bathes the brain and spinal cord. By detecting and correcting disturbances in the flow of this fluid, craniosacral therapists treat many different disorders affecting mind and body.

Feldenkrais is one of several types of bodywork. This method focuses on awareness of movement and utilizes the body as a primary learning vehicle. Feldenkrais practitioners rely on biomechanical principles and utilize both hands-on and mental imagery approaches to improve body functioning.

Herbalism has been a part of medical care for thousands of years. Plants contain many different substances which can alter physiology and mental states. Plant derived substances form the basis for many modern prescription drugs. Many native healers use herbalism in some form to treat a multitude of ailments.

Homeopathy utilizes minute concentrations of substances to treat a wide variety of illness. It is based on the principle that "like cures like". Thus, dilute solutions of substances which in high concentrations cause ailments similar to what are being treated, are given to effect cure. These solutions alter the flow of energy within the individual being treated in favorable ways.

Massage Therapies describe a number of different practices which involve touching, rubbing and applying pressure to different muscles and areas where muscles attach to bones. These manipulations help to relieve pain and stress and improve function. Massage is frequently very relaxing. Deep tissue, myofascial release, Swedish, and Shiatsu represent just a few of the many different types of massage.

Meditation involves a process to still or quiet the mind and enter into a state of awareness. There are many different techniques and schools of discipline which teach methods on how to enter this meditative state. Common focusing techniques emphasize concentrating on breathing or a particular point, or using a mantra. Other techniques utilize non-focusing techniques to promote meditation. More recently, high tech approaches using differential acoustic impulses help to facilitate meditation. Different states of meditation correlate with different brain wave activity. Meditation is believed to have beneficial physical, mental, and spiritual effects. Transcendental, Mindfulness, and Zen are three of the many types of meditation..

Moxibustion is part of traditional Chinese medicine. It involves burning an herb, mugwort, and placing the burning herb along specific points which direct the flow of *chi* (*qi*). These are analogous to the same points used in acupuncture. The intent is to remove blockages which are causing stagnation and prevent the normal flow of life energy.

Naturopathy represents an approach to healing widely used in Europe and the United States. Naturopaths recommend herbs and supplements to treat a wide variety of disorders. In addition, they may use nutritional approaches, acupuncture, various types of body work, and counseling. At the foundation of naturopathy is a belief that the body heals itself.

Osteopathy is founded on the belief that skeletal deformation and interference with adjacent nerves and blood vessels are the cause of most diseases. Osteopathy shares historical roots with Chiropractic. Both use manipulation to help correct skeletal deformities. Over time, in this country, osteopathic training has emphasized many of the same principles and practices of Allopathic Medicine.

Prayer as a healing strategy involves dialogue with God. Intercessory prayers ask for God or some deceased saint or person to intercede and enable healing to occur. Contemplative and Centering prayer are other types of prayer that represent specific meditative techniques.

Psychiatry is an Allopathic Medicine specialty which deals with emotional, cognitive, and behavioral disorders. Treatment modalities employed by psychiatry include the use of drugs and various therapies such as behavioral, cognitive, or rational emotive. Psychotherapy is a particular type of counseling approach which emphasizes a better personal understanding of the internal roots of illness.

Qi Gong is a component of traditional Chinese medicine. Techniques utilized include focusing on breathing, movement, visualization, and meditation. *Qi (Chi)* is life energy while *Gong (Kung)* means skill. The intent of these practices is to integrate body, mind, and spirit and bring balance.

Reflexology is a highly specific massage technique based on manipulating feet. Reflexologists believe that areas of the foot represent and control the flow of energy throughout the body. By carefully manipulating the feet, many different ailments can be treated and corrected.

Reiki represents an energy based healing modality which relies on *chakras,* energy vortices that correspond to areas along the spine and head. Different *chakras* are involved with various organs and body systems. These energy vortices may be over or under active resulting in some form of imbalance. A Reiki practitioner is able to recognize and correct these imbalances.

Rolfing employs techniques of deep massage to connective tissue in order to restore proper alignment, posture, and ease of movement. The focus is on improving physical function by removing some of the tightening in the muscles and connective tissue which often occur as a result of stress and poor body mechanics.

Social Activism means getting involved by contributing personal resources of time, money or effort into some cause to benefit society. Social activists are described as people who act as the voice or conscience of many individuals in society. By extending yourself into a cause bigger than yourself, a healing effect can occur.

Therapeutic Touch is based on the presence of a bioenergetic field encompassing each person. Disturbances in this field can be diagnosed and corrected through physical interaction by direct physical contact but more commonly by manipulation of the field surrounding an individual by the therapeutic touch practitioner.

Total Body Modification uses a specific muscle testing techniques, kinesiology, and bioenergetic principles to diagnose and correct imbalance of the organs and nervous system. A TBM practitioner may also use manipulations similar to Chiropractic to help correct these imbalances.

Traditional Chinese Medicine represents an ancient, comprehensive, integrated approach to treating illness and restoring health. *Chi,* vital energy, flows along different pathways called meridians. *Yin* and *Yang* are opposing forces of this vital energy which become imbalanced and cause illness. Different practices which include acupuncture, herbalism, qi gong, moxibustion, and meditation are all represented in Traditional Chinese Medicine. These and other techniques are designed to restore balance to body, mind, and spirit by optimizing the flow of *Yin* and *Yang.*

Volunteering as a healing strategy is any effort which involves donating time to a worthy cause. This provides opportunity for socialization and joining together in common cause to promote health and well-being. These efforts can be directed towards individuals, groups, organizations, neighborhood, community, or the world at large.

Yoga represents a multifaceted approach to health. It comes from an ancient Sanskrit word for union. Various physical postures, *asanas,* and focusing techniques such as regulated breathing and meditation are used to enhance physical fitness, focus the mind, and promote spiritual development. Yoga represents an entire philosophical approach to life with the ultimate goal of obtaining enlightenment. There are many different Yoga traditions; *hatha, sivananda,* and *ashtanga* are some representative disciplines.

Part Five:
Draw Your Map–Choose Your Path

Photo courtesy Paul Schnaittacher

This final section culminates all of your efforts to date. Having developed a broader, more comprehensive, integral understanding of your own health, and using the insights derived from completing the various health assessments, you are now ready to construct your map. This, after all, is what you have been waiting for and what I have been waiting for as well. The map that you create provides a representation of your integral health. It will help you chart a course to a place of better health. My role as your guide has been to lead you around the territory that is your health. By this time, you have explored the entire territory. If I have done my job, and you have been attentive, you now have a pretty good understanding of the lay of the land.

Thales said, "Know thyself." How can you best use your greater knowledge of self to enable you to realize your goal of improved health? **Self-transformation is the deepest type of self-care.** With greater understanding of yourself, you are empowered to make choices and decisions to achieve your goal. **No one can do this for you. No one will do this for you.** You have the ability to achieve better health. **The choice is yours...**

1. Describe what it means to you to be healthy:

_____

_____

2. What parts of yourself do you see as ill?

_____

_____

3. What parts of you do you see as healthy?

_____

_____

4. What physical issues are causing you pain/suffering?

_____

_____

5. What mental/emotional issues are causing you pain/suffering?

_____

_____

6. What spiritual issues are causing you pain/suffering?

_____

_____

7. What environmental issues (include relationships) are causing you pain/suffering?

_____

_____

8. Look in a mirror and study yourself for a few minutes.

In terms of your physical health, what do you see?

_____

_____

Look deeper to your mental and emotional health. What do you see?

_____

_____

Look deeper to the health of your soul and spirit. What do you see?

_____

_____

9. What connections do you make between disease and illness?

_____

_____

10. What connections do you make between pain and suffering?

_____

_____

11. What do you believe is wrong with you?

_____

_____

_____

_____

Review your 6 **Map Keys**. Pay particular attention to Map Key #1 and #6A (you should have been updating these throughout the various assessments).

Review your answers to the eleven questions above. Now list the most important health issues which you feel are affecting your health. List only one health issue per line. Your list can be as long or as short as you like. All of the items listed will be represented on your map. In the column on the right, indicate what part of you—body, mind, or spirit this issue affects the most.

Health Issue	Primarliy affects B, M, S

You are now ready to construct your health map:

Download and Print your Health Map and Action Plan—see Appendix

Or, get a large piece of paper; label the top, **"My Health Map"**

To draw your map, use the following three different axes:

North—South: Top of page = North; Bottom of page = South
This is your **Physical Axis**

East—West: Right side of page = East; Left side of page = West
This is your **Mental Axis**

Up—Down: On a two-dimensional surface this is represented by topography. Features with high elevations are things such as mountains, while valleys have low elevations. In this map use shading to demonstrate up/down.

High = light shading, Low = heavy shading
This is your Spiritual Axis

On this map, the further **North** you are, the better your **Physical** health. The further **East** you are, the better your **Mental** health. The **Higher** your elevation, the better your **Spiritual** health.

Draw a point on your map which best describes where you currently are on your **North—South (Body)** and **East—West (Mind)** **Axes.**

Trace a circle the size of a nickel around your point. Shade this area lightly or more heavily depending on how **High** (light shading) or **Low** (heavy shading) you feel best describes where you currently are on your **Spiritual** Axis.

Let's call this circle, "**A**". "A" represents where you currently stand with your overall health.

Now draw a point where you would like to be that is in a place of better health.

Trace a circle the size of a nickel around this second point and shade it according to where you want to be on your Spiritual Axis.

Call this second circle, "**B**". "B" represents your destination.

You are probably wondering, "How do I get from **A** to **B**"?
Use the following symbols to designate **Terrain Hazards:**

▲ Boulder blocking the way—A Physical obstacle

✗ ✗ Briar Patch—A Mental obstacle

✹ Swamp—A Spiritual obstacle

❖ Mud—A challenging Environment

Review the list of **Health Issues** you just completed. Use the **Terrain Symbols** above to represent each of the items on your list which you have designated as a health obstacle primarily affecting Body ▲ , Mind ✗ ✗, or Spirit ✹.

Symbolize each health issue you have listed and place it on your map with a short explanation about what issue each symbol represents. Draw these in red.

What resources do you have to help get you to your destination?

Consider important internal/external motivators, people, places, things you can do, and healing strategies which you want to use: (*refer to your assessments, Map Keys and Part 4*)

List these **Healing Resources** below: (The column to the right is for a corresponding map symbol which you will complete in a moment)

Healing Resource	Map Symbol

Your **Healing Resources** are places you can stop to get help along your journey.

᭬ Oasis—Where you spend time doing things which rest, rejuvenate, de-stress, and replenish you

✱ Scenic Vista—A place where you connect spiritually/nourish your soul

⌘ Garden—A place of forgiveness

▉ Community Center—Where you gather with family, friends and loved ones to enjoy and nurture relationships

🏛 House of Worship—Where you visit with God

⬤ Watering Hole—A place to quench your thirst and meet your body's needs

§ Supply Shop—Where you gather resources not available elsewhere

Match your **Healing Resource** symbols in the column above for Map Symbols.

Draw these symbols on your map in places along the way where you think you will need them the most. Draw these in green. Put a few words of explanation next to each symbol.

Put some muddy areas ❖ on your map. These represent challenging broad environmental issues which could arise from social, cultural, or physical environmental handicaps. Examples of "mud" could include growing up poor, or living in a high crime zone, or never completing your education, or coming from a dysfunctional family or home life. Draw these in brown and place a few words explaining what the mud represents.

You have completed your map. Congratulations, you have worked hard to come this far!

So how do you get from **A** to **B**? To the extent possible, you remove boulders, drain swamps, and cut down briar patches. When you are not able to do so, you try and go around these **Terrain Hazards.** When you can, you build a solid road over the muddy spots, but you trudge through the mud when you can't go over it. All along the way, stop as often as you can at your **Healing Resource** areas.

If your cartography skills are good, you are probably studying your map and charting your course. **Important Travel Advisory: The journey is much more important than**

the destination. If you focus on your journey, you will reach your destination sooner.

You are almost ready to head off. Before you go, ask yourself these last few questions. Think of this as a final checklist to review before you start. Put your answers on the flip side of your map. This will be your **Action Plan** to help you reach your destination.

1. **What specific paths (Body—Mind—Spirit—Environment) will I follow to reach my destination?**
2. **What blocks, obstacles, or difficulties (Body—Mind—Spirit—Environment) stand in my way?**
3. **What are my specific plans for dealing with these obstacles?**
4. **Who will assist me in my journey?**
5. **What is my timeline for arriving at my destination?**
6. **How will I gauge my progress along the way?**

Thus far, I have been your guide, but I believe you know your way around well enough to move ahead on your own. You made the map and it's a good one. It will help guide you along pathways to better health. If somewhere along the way you get lost, no problem! Just pull out your map, study it front and back, get your bearings, and resume your journey.

End of the Road

Linda Dawson is in her forties. She is vibrant and successful in the judgment of all who know her. She is a devoted mother and wife. With hard work, she has risen to the top of her career. At work she is liked and respected by most, envied by some. Linda is very health conscious; she is careful with her diet, exercises regularly, and maintains her ideal body weight. Linda is involved by volunteering at her church and in her community where she serves on various councils and committees. By all measures she appears to be in optimal health. In two weeks, she is scheduled to see her doctor for a regular checkup. Unknown to her, **Linda has breast cancer**.

The small lump her doctor discovered is, of course, some concern to her, but she has kept up with mammography and feels reassured that two years ago, she had found a lump which was biopsied and found to be benign. But this time is different. In a few days Linda's life changes when she gets the news that the biopsy she just had done revealed malignancy. **Linda has breast cancer**.

Two weeks later, Linda has had part of her breast removed and has started radiation treatment. Following her radiation she receives a course of chemotherapy. Her hair falls out. The treatments leave her feeling sick. She has never felt so tired. She is struggling at home. She has missed several important deadlines at work because of all the medical appointments she has to go to. She still goes to church but doesn't have the time or energy to volunteer. So too, she has given up all her community activities. By all measures, Linda is ill. But, the reality is, **Linda no longer has breast cancer**.

What is Linda's experience of disease? Is the presence or absence of her cancer a good measure of her health? Indeed, in the two weeks prior to her diagnosis she is in excellent health. Did her breast cancer change significantly two weeks later when she went to the doctor? No, the breast cancer hardly changed at all in those two weeks, but this is the point that Linda's health began to change. This was the beginning of her illness experience when she had to contend with fears that she could have cancer that she could die young, that her life could change. Two weeks later, the cancer hasn't changed much, but the news to Linda, that her biopsy is positive, has a huge impact. And weeks later, when technically, her breast cancer is gone, her illness has had a devastating effect.

Physically, she is drained and exhausted. Mentally, she can barely concentrate and is preoccupied. Emotionally, she is angry that her body has betrayed her in spite of her doing all the things she was supposed to. She fears her husband no longer finds her attractive and she worries about the future, especially if she will be around for her children. Spiritually, she has dropped all the things she used to do to nourish herself. She doesn't understand why God is punishing her in this way and questions her faith. Socially, most people around her feel sorry for her or are supportive. Secretly, some are glad to see her fallen, while others are thankful that it didn't happen to them. At a different level of society, her name has been entered into a cancer registry and she has simply become a statistic.

This example typifies how inadequate it is to consider health in terms of the presence or absence of disease. I like to think in terms of balance and energy. Throughout this book, I have encouraged you to think of the dynamic equilibrium between mind, body, spirit, and environment. It is the state of this equilibrium which characterizes the **illness experience**. It is this equilibrium which has gotten so out of balance in the example above. Typically, the doctor wants to take your illness experience and translate it into a diagnosis or label it as a disease. This characterizes it in a way that the science of medicine tells us how to treat you. **But in this scientific reductionism so much is lost**.

In truth, the illness experience is unique to each individual. Medicine, as a scientific discipline is much less concerned about individuals and much more so with large study groups or cohorts of patients. By lumping together large groups of people who share a common diagnosis, we can examine the effectiveness of a new medicine or compare different treatment approaches to the same disease. Such an approach has yielded dramatic advances in treating and curing diseases. But it has also contributed to a depersonalization of mainstream medical care. In the case of Linda, her breast cancer is cured, but she is far from being restored to health. Much of what constitutes her illness experience, much of what really needs to be treated is not as easily studied through scientific investigation and is all too often overlooked as part of the care she receives. And so it goes with almost every diagnosis. **It is much easier to focus on treatment of a diagnosis than it is to understand an individual and treat their illness in an integral way.**

Let me give you another example, taken from a recent study just published in a major medical journal. Researchers examined a cohort of patients who suffered from chronic daily headaches and investigated using different strengths of botulinum toxin *(BOTOX)*. Since many of these headaches are caused by muscular contraction and botulinum toxin injections cause muscular relaxation this certainly is a very rational and scientific treatment approach. I am not disputing that such a treatment approach can be beneficial. I am, however, troubled by the notion that this is how we should approach treatment of chronic daily headache. Every member of that study cohort and every person who suffers from chronic daily headache is a unique individual. The reasons for their headache and their individual illness experience are different. **How can we treat them all the same way?** If our approach does not comprehensively asses patients as individuals, how is it determined how best to care for each individual?

A starting point is to begin to think about the illness experience for that person. Lots of probing questions and assistance with self-inquiry and introspection will likely uncover a wealth of information which can ultimately restore that person to health. **Isn't that what we are all after, a restoration of health? Balance?**

When care is approached in this manner, it is evident that the illness experience is really wrapped up and entangled by all the attachments that accompany diagnoses. Some of these lead up into the diagnosis, e.g. feeling stressed out by unruly kids which results in a muscle contraction headache. Some of these entanglements flow from the diagnosis, e.g. feeling worried about the future because you just got diagnosed with breast cancer. In the **Integral** approach, we begin to explore where these attachments are. When you disentangle some of these connections, you can begin to appreciate the significance of a diagnosis for yourself as an individual and to develop a more comprehensive understanding of your health. It is my sincere hope that the contents of this guidebook have started you on a journey towards such a better understanding of your health.

Where do you stand on the spectrum from wellness to illness? Can you begin to disconnect some of the unhealthy things which are attached to your diagnoses, whatever they may be? Can you make new connections which might offer you a pathway to grow personally, or adopt new healthier perspectives? **Disease to which no significance is attached has no power to influence health**. Can you see yourself from an integral perspective and see how you can travel to a place of improved balance and wholeness?

Ultimately, the choice is yours. The tools and information given are very empowering. Hopefully you have gained a richer, more comprehensive understanding of your own health. You have created a representative map which details the territory of your health. This knowledge can take you down a path of better health and help you to regain energetic balance.

Mind, body, and spirit are all in some complex dynamic interplay in each and every one of us. These components are in dynamic equilibrium (or not) with one another and with the world around us. This environment is rich in complexity and includes much more than just the physical space around us. The shared values, beliefs and language that represent culture, as well as a panoply of socioeconomic factors also occupy our environment. These are the elements that constitute our reality. All of these elements are represented in Ken Wilber's Integral Model, which effectively provides us with a map to understand ourselves and the world—to understand our reality. All of these elements play a part in our health.

Medicine has evolved into primarily a scientific discipline. As such, it focuses more on the treatment of disease than on individuals. The natural history of disease processes and treatments which can favorably influence these processes are amenable to scientific investigation. These treatments are grounded in science. This is good. Medicine should be grounded on a solid foundation of scientific rationale and proof. But, this has been bad for medical care. Care has focused more on the disease and less on the person who is experiencing that disease. Medical care has focused less on assessment and more on treatment. Medical care has become fragmented with a host of different practitioners offering a maze of different mainstream, complementary, and integrative therapies. How do you choose from the many alternatives?

I believe the integral approach provides the answer. Examining the unique aspects of an individual and comprehensively assessing a person is the first step to determining a treatment plan. It starts with you, because in some sense, "It's all about you." What makes you the unique person that you are? How is this all wrapped up in your health? How can you realize your goal of feeling better and enjoying better health and well-being?

Some readers may have been surprised to see my inclusion of voluntarism and social activism in the section on healing strategies. At times, I have felt the best prescription I could offer a patient was to have them make brownies for their church bake sale, or spend some time dishing out meals in a community soup kitchen. Participating in something bigger than our individual selves seems to have a healing and therapeutic effect. There exists an interrelatedness to healing such that doing something to heal others contributes to our own healing. A criticism I have levied throughout this book is that health care has become terribly fragmented. But the same criticism can be applied to the notion of each person having a separate, body, mind, and spirit. The same criticism applies to the notion that we are separate individuals living in a complex world subject to various social and cultural forces and influences. Such distinctions are in and of themselves fragmentary and therefore not integral.

A truly integral approach recognizes that all of these different aspects are part of a whole. If you believe that the beating of butterfly wings contributes to hurricanes than you have this understanding of the interconnectedness we share. You have no separate body, mind, or spirit and you are not separate from the whole of the world or the entire Kosmos for that matter. Your health, my health, the health of humanity and of the planet is all integrally connected. Healing at this level is a challenge that we all share. Vimala Thakar has stated this so eloquently:

As we deepen in understanding, the arbitrary divisions between inner and outer disappear. The essence of life, the beauty and grandeur of life, is in it wholeness. Life in reality cannot be divided into the inner and the outer, the individual and social. We may make arbitrary divisions for the convenience of collective life, for analysis, but essentially any division between inner and outer has no reality, no meaning. *Spirituality and Social Action: A Holistic Approach*

So where does this leave us? Together you and I have traveled in the pages of this guidebook. Thank you for your company and thank you for your attention as I have tried to point out the territory that represents health. It's a pretty big territory with lots of pitfalls, hazards, and obstacles. Places and opportunities for healing abound. There are quite a few signs around to help you figure out where you are headed, but you need to know how to read them. Hopefully you now have a better lay of the land and know what supplies you need to get where you are going. While this is my end of the road with you, your journey goes on. The pathways are yours to choose as you make your way around this territory. The journey continues for the rest of your life. Explore. Have fun. Take some risks. Enjoy the scenery. At all times, may you travel in and to a place of health, of healing, of wholeness, and of balance…

Photo courtesy Paul Schnaittacher

Parting Words

These words, written by one of my instructors, move me in a profound way. I share them with you:

The goal of an Integral Medicine is to utilize our fully developed inner and outer healing capacities to attain an end to all suffering (physical, emotional, existential and conditioned) and to promote the natural development of Human Flourishing—a reconfiguration and transformation of our current understanding of health and healing. This new vision and its approaches embrace the achievements of an outer medicine yet are uniquely characterized by the further attainment of a personal and deeply felt sense of wholeness, peace, joy and love—in their immediacy and presence.

Elliott Dacher, M.D., *Institute of Noetic Sciences Retreat on "Consciousness and Healing", April, 2005*

Photo courtesy Paul Schnaittacher

VIDEO LINK #5 IN APPENDIX

My Health Map

Terrain Hazards:

- ▶ Boulder blocking the way—A Physical obstacle
- ✕✕ Briar Patch—A Mental obstacle
- ▦ Swamp—A Spiritual obstacle
- ❖ Mud—A challenging Environment

Healing Resources:

- ✿ Oasis—Where you spend time doing things which rest, rejuvenate, de-stress, and replenish you
- ✹ Scenic Vista—A place where you connect spiritually/nourish
- ⌘ Garden—A place of forgiveness
- ▪ Community Center—Where you gather with family, friends and loved ones to enjoy and nurture relationships
- ⛪ House of Worship—Where you visit with God
- ● Watering Hole—A place to quench your thirst and meet your body's needs
- ⚖ Supply Shop—Where you gather resources not available elsewhere

Date: *My Action Plan*

1. What specific paths (Body-Mind-Spirit-Environment) will I follow to reach my destination?

2. What blocks, obstacles,, or difficulties (Body-Mind-Spirit-Environment) stand in my way?

3. What are my specific plans for dealing with these obstacles?

4. Who will assist me in my journey?

5. What is my timeline for arriving at my destination?

6. How will I gauge my progress along the way?

Appendix

Additional content for readers is available as hyperlinks for e-book readers. This same material is available online at **www.pathstohealth.info**. This web-based material is designed to enhance the reading experience. The text identifies where this material is best referenced as follows:

Introduction Video link #1:

Video Link # 2

Video Link #3

Video Link #4

Download and print Map Key Assessments

1st Map Key video

2nd Map Key video

3rd Map Key video

4th Map key video

5th Map Key video

6th Map Key video

Download and Print your Health Map and Action Plan

Parting Words Video link #5

CPSIA information can be obtained at www.ICGtesting.com
Printed in the USA
LVOW05s1827010215

425250LV00013B/576/P